FAMILY ISSUES IN THE 21ST CENTURY

U.S. FAMILY PLANNING AND POPULATION ASSISTANCE ABROAD

POLICIES AND RESTRICTIONS

FAMILY ISSUES IN THE 21ST CENTURY

Additional books in this series can be found on Nova's website under the Series tab.

Additional E-books in this series can be found on Nova's website under the E-book tab.

FAMILY ISSUES IN THE 21ST CENTURY

U.S. FAMILY PLANNING AND POPULATION ASSISTANCE ABROAD

POLICIES AND RESTRICTIONS

ELVA A. RIVERA
AND
DELORIS R. MURPHY
EDITORS

New York

For permission to use material from this book please contact us:
Telephone 631-231-7269; Fax 631-231-8175
Web Site: http://www.novapublishers.com

Library of Congress Cataloging-in-Publication Data

ISBN: 978-1-62618-532-6

Published by Nova Science Publishers, Inc. † New York

CONTENTS

PREFACE

This book examines the current policies and restrictions relating to U.S. family planning and population assistance abroad. Topics discussed in this book include abortion and family planning-related provisions in U.S. foreign assistance law and policy; international family planning programs; and background information on the U.N. Population Fund and U.S. funding debate.

Chapter 1 – This report details legislation and policies that restrict or place requirements on U.S. funding of abortion or family planning activities abroad. The level and extent of federal funding for these activities is an ongoing and controversial issue in U.S. foreign assistance and will likely continue to be a point of contention during the 113th Congress.

These issues have been debated for over four decades in the context of a broader domestic abortion controversy that began with the Supreme Court's 1973 ruling in *Roe v. Wade*, which holds that the Constitution protects a woman's decision to terminate her pregnancy. Since Roe, Congress has enacted foreign assistance legislation placing restrictions or requirements on the federal funding of abortions and on family planning activities abroad. Many of these provisions, often referred to by the name of the lawmakers that introduced them, have been included in foreign aid authorizations, appropriations, or both, and affect different types of foreign assistance. Examples include

- the "**Helms amendment**," which prohibits the use of U.S. funds to perform abortions or to coerce individuals to practice abortions;

- the "**Biden amendment**," which states that U.S. funds may not be used for biomedical research related to abortion or involuntary sterilization;
- the "**Siljander amendment**," which prohibits U.S. funds from being used to lobby for or against abortion;
- the "**Kemp-Kasten amendment**," which prohibits funding for any organization or program that, as determined by the President, supports or participates in the management of a program of coercive abortion or involuntary sterilization; and
- the "**Tiahrt amendment**," which places requirements on voluntary family planning projects receiving assistance from USAID.

The executive branch has also engaged in the debate over international abortion and family planning. In 1984, President Ronald Reagan issued what has become known as the "Mexico City policy," which required foreign non-governmental organizations receiving USAID family planning assistance to certify that they would not perform or actively promote abortion as a method of family planning, even if such activities were conducted with non-U.S. funds. The policy was rescinded by President Bill Clinton and reinstituted by President George W. Bush. It was rescinded by President Barack Obama in January 2009 and remains a controversial issue in U.S. foreign assistance.

This report focuses primarily on legislative restrictions and executive branch policies related to international abortion and family planning.

Chapter 2 – Since 1965, the U.S. government has supported international family planning activities based on principles of voluntarism and informed choice that gives participants access to services and information on a broad range of family planning methods. U.S. family planning policy and abortion restrictions have generated contentious debate for over three decades, resulting in frequent clarification and modification of U.S. international family planning programs. Given the divisive nature of this debate, U.S. funding of these programs will likely remain a point of contention during the 112th Congress.

In 1984, controversy arose over U.S. family planning assistance when the Ronald Reagan Administration introduced restrictions that became known as the "Mexico City policy." The Mexico City policy required foreign non-governmental organizations (NGOs) to certify that they would not perform or actively promote abortion as a method of family planning—even if the activities were undertaken with non-U.S. funds. Presidents Reagan and George H. W. Bush also suspended grants to the U.N. Population Fund (UNFPA) due to evidence of coercive family planning practices in China, citing violations of the "Kemp-Kasten" amendment, which bans U.S. assistance to organizations that, as determined by the President, support or participate in the management of coercive family planning programs.

President Bill Clinton resumed UNFPA funding and rescinded the Mexico City policy in 1993. In 2001, however, President George W. Bush reapplied the Mexico City policy restrictions. The Bush Administration also suspended U.S. contributions to UNFPA from FY2002 to FY2008 following a State Department investigation of family planning programs in China. In January 2009, President Barack Obama issued a memorandum rescinding the Mexico City policy. The President also stated that the United States would resume U.S. contributions to UNFPA.

Recent international family planning-related appropriations and Obama Administration requests are outlined below.

- **FY2013—**In February 2012, President Obama requested a total of **$642.7 million** in international family planning and reproductive health (FP/RH) funding, including **$39 million** for UNFPA.
- **FY2012—**In December 2011, President Obama signed the Consolidated Appropriations Act, 2012 (P.L. 112-74), which directs that not less than **$575 million** should be made available for FP/RH activities. It also states that **$35 million** shall be made available for UNFPA.
- **FY2011—**FY2011 appropriations for international family planning and reproductive health are included in the Department of Defense and Full-Year Continuing Appropriations Act, 2011 (P.L. 112-10), which directs that not less that **$575 million** should be made available for international FP/RH activities. It also allocated **$40 million** for UNFPA.

Chapter 3 – The United Nations Population Fund (UNFPA), established in 1969, is the world's largest source of population and reproductive health programs and the principal unit within the United Nations for global population issues. In 2009, the organization provided services in 155 developing and transition countries, with funds totaling $783.1 million, drawn primarily from voluntary contributions made by nations and some foundations.

The United States, with strong support from Congress, was an important actor in the launch of UNFPA in 1969. During the mid-to-late 1960s, Congress began to express heightened concern over the impact of rapid population growth on development prospects in poor countries. In 1967, Congress earmarked funds for population assistance programs, urging the United States to channel family planning resources through the United Nations and other international organizations.

Since it was established, UNFPA has transitioned from an organization focused on statistical collection and analysis to an agency providing maternal and child health/family planning assistance. UNFPA played a large role in shaping the 1994 International Conference on Population and Development, held in Cairo. The Cairo Conference marked a turning point in the international debate over the impact of population issues on global development, and established a policy framework called the Plan of Action that continues to guide current family planning and reproductive health policies, including the work of UNFPA. The Plan integrated population concerns into the broad context of development—concluding that education and health, including reproductive health, were prerequisites for sustainable development.

In the past three decades, there has been continuing and contentious debate within the United States, especially among Members of Congress, as to whether the United States should financially support UNFPA. This debate has centered on the extent to which, if any, UNFPA aids China's coercive family planning programs and policies. In 15 of the past 25 years, the United States did not contribute to the organization as a result of executive branch determinations that UNFPA's program in China violated the "Kemp-Kasten" amendment, which bans U.S. aid to organizations involved in the management of coercive family planning programs. From FY2002 through FY2008, the George W. Bush Administration found UNFPA ineligible for funding under the Kemp-Kasten amendment.

In March 2009, President Barack Obama expressed his support for UNFPA and announced that the United States would contribute $50 million to the organization as directed in the Omnibus Appropriations Act, 2009 (P.L. 111-8). On December 16, 2009, President Obama signed the Consolidated Appropriations Act, 2010 (P.L. 111-117). Division F of that bill, the Department of State, Foreign Operations, and Related Programs Appropriations Act, 2010, directed that $55 million should be made available for UNFPA. For FY2011, the Obama Administration requested $50 million for U.S. contributions to UNFPA, which would be drawn from the International Organizations and Programs account (IO&P).

While UNFPA receives voluntary contributions from many countries and some private foundations, most of its income comes from a handful of donors. The Netherlands, Sweden, and Japan have consistently been the largest contributors. In 2009, the U.S. contribution to UNFPA was the fourth-largest donation, representing approximately 9.5% of UNFPA's annual regular budget.

In: U.S. Family Planning ...
Editors: E.A. Rivera and D.R. Murphy ISBN: 978-1-62618-532-6

Chapter 1

ABORTION AND FAMILY PLANNING-RELATED PROVISIONS IN U.S. FOREIGN ASSISTANCE LAW AND POLICY*

Luisa Blanchfield

SUMMARY

This report details legislation and policies that restrict or place requirements on U.S. funding of abortion or family planning activities abroad. The level and extent of federal funding for these activities is an ongoing and controversial issue in U.S. foreign assistance and will likely continue to be a point of contention during the 113th Congress.

These issues have been debated for over four decades in the context of a broader domestic abortion controversy that began with the Supreme Court's 1973 ruling in *Roe v. Wade*, which holds that the Constitution protects a woman's decision to terminate her pregnancy. Since Roe, Congress has enacted foreign assistance legislation placing restrictions or requirements on the federal funding of abortions and on family planning activities abroad. Many of these provisions, often referred to by the name of the lawmakers that introduced them, have been included in foreign aid authorizations,

* This is an edited, reformatted and augmented version of the Congressional Research Service Publication, CRS Report for Congress R41360, dated February 12, 2013.

appropriations, or both, and affect different types of foreign assistance. Examples include

- the "**Helms amendment**," which prohibits the use of U.S. funds to perform abortions or to coerce individuals to practice abortions;
- the "**Biden amendment**," which states that U.S. funds may not be used for biomedical research related to abortion or involuntary sterilization;
- the "**Siljander amendment**," which prohibits U.S. funds from being used to lobby for or against abortion;
- the "**Kemp-Kasten amendment**," which prohibits funding for any organization or program that, as determined by the President, supports or participates in the management of a program of coercive abortion or involuntary sterilization; and
- the "**Tiahrt amendment**," which places requirements on voluntary family planning projects receiving assistance from USAID.

The executive branch has also engaged in the debate over international abortion and family planning. In 1984, President Ronald Reagan issued what has become known as the "Mexico City policy," which required foreign non-governmental organizations receiving USAID family planning assistance to certify that they would not perform or actively promote abortion as a method of family planning, even if such activities were conducted with non-U.S. funds. The policy was rescinded by President Bill Clinton and reinstituted by President George W. Bush. It was rescinded by President Barack Obama in January 2009 and remains a controversial issue in U.S. foreign assistance.

This report focuses primarily on legislative restrictions and executive branch policies related to international abortion and family planning.

INTRODUCTION

One of the most controversial issues in U.S. foreign assistance concerns restrictions on U.S. funding for abortion and family planning activities abroad. For many, the debate focuses on three key questions:

- Do countries or organizations that receive U.S. assistance perform abortions or engage in coercive abortion or involuntary sterilization activities with U.S. funds?

- Should U.S. funding be permitted or withheld from countries or organizations that participate in these activities?
- What impact, if any, might the withholding of U.S. funds have on population growth, family planning, and reproductive health services in developing countries?

Members of Congress have engaged in heated debates regarding these issues in connection with a broader domestic controversy regarding U.S. abortion policy. These debates have continued since the Supreme Court's 1973 landmark ruling in *Roe v. Wade*, which holds that the Constitution protects a woman's decision whether to terminate her pregnancy.[1] In every Congress since *Roe*, Members who oppose abortion have introduced legislation that would prohibit the practice in the United States. Many congressional opponents have also sought to attach provisions to annual appropriations measures banning the use of federal funds to perform abortions.

Before the *Roe* decision, the majority of discussions in Congress regarding the federal funding of abortion focused on domestic authorization and appropriations legislation, particularly labor and health and human services appropriations. After *Roe*, however, the controversy spread to U.S. foreign assistance, leading to the enactment of abortion and voluntary family planning restrictions in foreign assistance authorizations and appropriations.

Debate over international abortion restrictions has also reached the executive branch. In 1984, President Reagan issued what has become known as the "Mexico City policy," which required foreign non-governmental organizations (NGOs) receiving U.S. Agency for International Development (USAID) family planning assistance to certify that they would not perform or actively promote abortion as a method of family planning, even if such activities were undertaken with non-U.S. funds.[2] In the intervening years, the Mexico City policy has been rescinded and reissued by various Administrations. Most recently, it was rescinded by President Barack Obama in January 2009.

During the 112th Congress, Members continued to debate prohibitions and restrictions on abortion and family planning activities abroad. As in prior appropriations cycles, some Members sought to renew, add, modify, or remove language addressing these issues in State-Foreign Operations legislation. Some also introduced legislation aiming to make the Mexico City policy, or its reversal, permanent law. Federal funding for abortion and family planning activities remains a controversial issue in foreign assistance, and congressional interest in the subject is expected to extend into the 113th Congress.

This report examines key legislative and executive branch policies that restrict or place requirements on U.S. funding of abortion or voluntary family planning activities abroad. It discusses when and how the policies were introduced and the types of foreign aid to which they apply. Further information on U.S. family planning assistance, including U.S. funding levels and USAID activities, is included in *International Family Planning Programs: Issues for Congress*, by Luisa Blanchfield.[3]

SETTING THE CONTEXT: LEGISLATIVE VEHICLES

Many of the restrictions attached to U.S. funding of abortion and requirements relating to voluntary family planning programs abroad are included in foreign aid authorizations, appropriations, or both, and affect different types of foreign assistance. Some provisions have come to be known by the name of the lawmakers who introduced them (for example, the "Helms amendment"), while others are identified by the subjects they address (for example, "involuntary sterilization").

Legislation that authorizes foreign aid establishes, continues, or modifies an agency or program for a fixed or indefinite period of time. The Foreign Assistance Act of 1961 (FAA), as amended, is the cornerstone of permanent foreign aid authorization law.[4]

The FAA is divided into several "parts" that authorize different types of foreign assistance, including development assistance (part I); military and security assistance (part II); general, administrative, and miscellaneous provisions (part III); the Enterprise for the Americas Initiative (part IV); and debt reduction for developing countries with tropical forests (part V). Congress has routinely amended the FAA since 1961 and has authorized new programs in stand-alone acts, but it has not comprehensively reauthorized most programs in the FAA since 1985. Subsequent authorization bills have often stalled in the face of debates and disagreements on controversial issues (including abortion and family planning), a tight legislative calendar, or foreign policy disputes between Congress and the executive branch.

In the absence of the regular enactment of foreign aid authorizations, Congress has annually considered appropriations measures that set spending levels for nearly every foreign assistance account. In recent years, these measures have become increasingly significant for Congress in influencing how U.S. foreign aid is disbursed. Many of them have included family planning or abortion-related restrictions or requirements.[5]

The links among the various requirements and restrictions, as well as their inclusion in different legislation, are complex and in some cases not immediately apparent. For example, some amendments that were already enacted in the FAA, such as the Helms and Biden provisions, appear to be added to other foreign assistance-related legislation for emphasis.[6] In other cases, the provisions may have been added so that they apply to additional categories of foreign aid not covered under the FAA. Moreover, some restrictions and requirements stand on their own, while others seek to clarify and amend other existing restrictions. The Leahy amendment, for instance, defines the term "motivate" as written in the Helms amendment, while the Livingston amendment seeks to clarify prohibitions in the DeConcini amendment.

Current Restrictions or Requirements in Legislation

This section details enacted legislative restrictions relating to U.S. funding of abortion and requirements related to voluntary family planning programs abroad. They are listed in chronological order by the year they were enacted.

A Note about FY2013 Foreign Operations Appropriations

Several abortion and family planning-related restrictions discussed in this report are included in annual foreign operations appropriations bills. Fiscal year (FY) 2013 appropriations are currently operating under the Continuing Appropriations Resolution, FY2013 (H.J.Res. 117, P.L. 112-175), which was approved by Congress on September 28, 2012, and will expire on March 27, 2013.

Under the continuing resolution, all restrictions and conditions from the Department of State, Foreign Operations, and Related Programs Appropriations Act, 2012 continue to apply.[7]

Helms Amendment (1973)

The Helms amendment prohibits the use of U.S. foreign assistance funds to perform abortions or to motivate or coerce individuals to practice abortions. Introduced by Senator Jesse Helms in 1973, it was adopted as an amendment to the FAA because of concerns that federal funds could be used to perform abortions overseas. Under the FAA heading "Prohibition on Use of Funds for Abortions and Involuntary Sterilizations," the Helms amendment states:

(1) None of the funds made available to carry this part may be used to pay for the performance of abortions as a method of family planning or to motivate or coerce any person to practice abortions.[8]

The amendment as written in the FAA applies to all foreign assistance activities authorized by part I of that act (development assistance).

Since FY1980, the Helms amendment has also periodically been enacted in foreign operations appropriations measures.[9] It is included in two places in the Department of State, Foreign Operations, and Related Programs Appropriations Act, 2012 (hereafter referred to as the "FY2012 State-Foreign Operations Appropriations Act").[10] In Section 7018 of Title VII, General Provisions, the language applies to all foreign assistance activities in the act that are authorized under part I of the FAA (development assistance).[11] In Title III, Bilateral Economic Assistance, the language applies to foreign assistance activities in the entire act.[12]

Involuntary Sterilization (1978)

In 1978, Congress passed an amendment to the FAA specifying that U.S. foreign assistance may not fund (1) the performance of involuntary sterilizations, or (2) the coercion of involuntary sterilizations (or provide financial incentives to undergo sterilization):

> None of the funds made available to carry out this part may be used to pay for the performance of involuntary sterilizations as a method of family planning or to coerce or provide any financial incentive to any person to undergo sterilizations.[13]

The provision is also repeated in annual foreign operations appropriations. Most recently, it was included in Section 7018 of the FY2012 State-Foreign Operations Appropriations Act.[14] In both the FAA and State-Foreign Operations appropriations acts, it applies to all foreign assistance activities authorized by part I of the FAA (development assistance).

Peace Corps (1978)

Since FY1979, annual foreign operations appropriations have included abortion restrictions on Peace Corps funding. Under the heading "Peace Corps" in the FY2012 State-Foreign Operations Appropriations Act, for example, it states that "none of the funds appropriated under this heading shall be used to pay for abortions."[15] The provision was enacted in response to reports that money appropriated to the Peace Corps was being used to finance abortions for Peace Corps personnel.[16] The amendment applies only to U.S. financing of the Peace Corps.

No restrictions exist on funding for the medical evacuation of Peace Corps volunteers who decide to have an abortion. Under existing policy, the Peace Corps covers the cost of evacuation to a location where "medically adequate facilities" for obtaining an abortion are available and where abortions are legally permissible.[17]

Biden Amendment (1981)

In 1981, Congress passed an amendment to the FAA specifying that the United States may not provide foreign assistance for biomedical research related to abortion or involuntary sterilization. This provision, named after Senator Joseph Biden, states:

> None of the funds made available to carry out this part may be used to pay for any biomedical research which relates, in whole or in part, to methods of, or the performance of, abortions or involuntary sterilization as a means of family planning.[18]

The Biden amendment has also been included in foreign operations appropriations acts. Most recently, it was included in Section 7018 of the FY2012 State-Foreign Operations Appropriations Act.[19] The provision as included in the FAA and the FY2012 State-Foreign Operations Appropriations Act applies to all foreign assistance activities authorized by part I of the FAA (development assistance).

Siljander Amendment (1981)

In 1981, Representative Mark Siljander introduced an amendment to the FY1982 Foreign Assistance and Related Programs Appropriations Act specifying that no U.S. funds may be used to lobby for abortion.[20] Since the Siljander amendment was first introduced, Congress has modified the amendment to state that no funds may be used to "lobby for *or against* abortion" (emphasis added).

The Siljander amendment has been included in annual foreign operations appropriations acts.[21] It applies to all programs and activities appropriated under such acts. Most recently, the FY2012 State-Foreign Operations Appropriations Act states that "none of the funds made available under this Act may be used to lobby for or against abortion."[22]

DeConcini Amendment (1985)

In 1985, Congress enacted a provision to the FY1986 Foreign Assistance and Related Programs Appropriations Act specifying that the United States would only fund family planning projects that offer a range of family planning methods and services, either directly or through referral.[23] The measure was enacted to counter a Reagan Administration policy that would provide U.S. funding to overseas groups that advocate only "natural" family planning methods and services, such as abstinence.[24] The amendment, introduced by Senator Dennis DeConcini, states:

> That in order to reduce reliance on abortion in developing nations, funds shall be available only to family planning projects which offer, either directly or through referral to, or information about access to, a broad range of family planning methods and services.[25]

The provision has been included in annual foreign operations appropriations legislation since 1985, and it is most recently included in the

FY2012 State-Foreign Operations Appropriations Act.[26] It is applied to family planning assistance funded through all accounts under that act.

Additional Provision on Involuntary Sterilization and Abortion (1985)

In 1985, Congress included a provision in the FY1986 Foreign Assistance and Related Programs Appropriations Act requiring that no funds made available under part I of the FAA may be obligated for any given country or organization if the President certifies that the use of such funds violates the aforementioned Helms, Biden, or involuntary sterilization amendments.[27] The amendment states:

> None of the funds made available to carry out part I of the Foreign Assistance Act of 1961, as amended, may be obligated or expended for any country or organization if the President certifies that the use of these funds by any such country or organization would violate any of the above provisions related to abortions or involuntary sterilizations [the Helms, Biden, and involuntary sterilization amendments].[28]

The provision has been included in annual foreign operations appropriations. Most recently, it is incorporated into the FY2012 State-Foreign Operations Appropriations Act.[29] It applies to all foreign assistance activities in the act that are authorized under part I of the FAA (development assistance).

Kemp-Kasten Amendment (1985)

In 1985, Congress agreed to the Kemp-Kasten amendment as part of the FY1985 Supplemental Appropriations Act.[30] The measure, introduced by Senator Bob Kasten and Representative Jack Kemp, states:

> None of the funds made available under this Act nor any unobligated balances from prior appropriations Acts may be made available to any organization or program which, as determined by the President, supports or participates in the management of a program of coercive abortion or involuntary sterilization.[31]

The provision was adopted due to the concerns of President Reagan and some Members of Congress that the U.N. Population Fund's (UNFPA's) program in China engaged in or provided funding for abortion or coercive family planning programs.[32] It has been included in annual foreign operations appropriations legislation measures since FY1985. Most recently, it is included in the FY2012 State-Foreign Operations Appropriations Act.[33] Although it applies to any organization or program that supports or participates in coercive abortion or involuntary sterilization, a determination has only been made regarding UNFPA.

In 15 of the past 26 years, the United States has not contributed to UNFPA as a result of executive branch determinations that UNFPA's program in China violated the Kemp-Kasten amendment. For seven years, the George W. Bush Administration transferred funds appropriated for UNFPA to other foreign aid activities. The Obama Administration, however, has supported U.S. funding for the organization. In March 2009, a State Department spokesperson confirmed that the U.S. government would contribute $50 million to UNFPA as provided by the FY2009 Department of State, Foreign Operations, and Related Programs Appropriations Act.[34] This decision, according to Administration officials, highlighted the President's "strong commitment" to international family planning, women's health, and global development.[35] In FY2012, the United States contributed $35 million to UNFPA.

In recent years, in response to concerns regarding UNFPA's program in China and in addition to Kemp-Kasten restrictions, Congress has enacted certain conditions for U.S. funding of UNFPA. Most recently, Section 7085 of the FY2012 State-Foreign Operations Appropriations Act requires that

- funds not made available for UNFPA because of any provision of law shall be transferred to the Global Health Programs account and made available for family planning, maternal, and reproductive health activities;
- none of the funds made available to UNFPA may be used by UNFPA for a country program in China;
- U.S. contributions to UNFPA be kept in an account segregated from other UNFPA accounts and not be commingled with other sums; and for UNFPA to receive U.S. funding, it cannot fund abortions.

The act also required the Secretary of State to submit a report to the committees on appropriations on dollar-for-dollar withholding of funds. Specifically, not later than four months after the enactment of P.L. 112-74, the

Secretary is required to submit a report to the committees on appropriations indicating the funds UNFPA is budgeting for a country program in China. If the Secretary's report states that funds will be spent on such a program, then the amount of such funds shall be deducted from the funds made available to UNFPA for the remainder of the fiscal year in which the report is submitted.[36]

Livingston Amendment (1986)

In 1986, Representative Bob Livingston introduced an amendment as part of FY1987 continuing appropriations that prohibited the United States from discriminating against organizations based on their religious or conscientious commitment to offer only "natural" family planning when awarding related grants:

> [I]n awarding grants for natural family planning under section 104 of the Foreign Assistance Act no applicants shall be discriminated against because of such applicant's religious or conscientious commitment to offer only natural family planning; and, additionally, all such applicants shall comply with the requirements of the previous proviso [DeConcini amendment].[37]

The Livingston amendment is related to the DeConcini amendment, which states that the United States shall only fund family planning projects that offer a range of family planning methods and services, either directly or through referral. The measure ensures that the United States cannot discriminate against organizations that support natural family planning methods when awarding family planning grants and agreements, providing such organizations comply with the DeConcini amendment.

The provision has been included in foreign operations appropriations, and it is most recently incorporated into the FY2012 State-Foreign Operations Appropriations Act.[38] It is applied to family planning assistance from any account appropriated under that act.

Leahy Amendment (1994)

The Leahy amendment, introduced by Senator Patrick Leahy in 1994 as an amendment to the FY1995 Foreign Operations, Export Financing, and Related Programs Appropriations Act, seeks to clarify language in the Helms amendment, which states, "None of the funds made available ... may be used to pay for the performance of abortions as a method of family planning or to *motivate* or coerce any person to practice abortions" (emphasis added).[39] The Leahy provision aims to address some policymakers' concerns that providing information or counseling about all legal pregnancy options could potentially be viewed as violating the Helms amendment. The most recent version states:

> [F]or purposes of this or any other Act authorizing or appropriating funds for the Department of State, foreign operations, and related programs, the term ''motivate,'' as it relates to family planning assistance, shall not be construed to prohibit the provision, consistent with local law, of information or counseling about all pregnancy options.[40]

The amendment has been included in foreign operations appropriations in various forms since it first appeared in enacted legislation. It is currently included in the FY2012 State-Foreign Operations Appropriations Act, and applies to all enacted authorization and appropriations legislation related to the Department of State, foreign operations, and related programs.

Tiahrt Amendment (1998)

In October 1998, Congress enacted an amendment introduced by Representative Todd Tiahrt as part of the FY1999 Foreign Operations, Export Financing, and Related Programs Appropriations Act that directs voluntary family planning projects supported by the United States to comply with five specific requirements.[41] The provision, which became known as the Tiahrt amendment, has been included in foreign operations appropriations in each subsequent fiscal year. It states that "funds shall be made available" only to voluntary family planning projects that meet the following requirements:

> (1) service providers or referral agents in the project shall not implement or be subject to quotas, or other numerical targets, of total number of births, number of family planning acceptors, or acceptors of a particular method of family planning (this provision shall not be construed to include the use of quantitative estimates or indicators for budgeting and planning purposes);
>
> (2) the project shall not include payment of incentives, bribes, gratuities, or financial reward to: (A) an individual in exchange for becoming a family planning acceptor; or (B) program personnel for achieving a numerical target

or quota of total number of births, number of family planning acceptors, or acceptors of a particular method of family planning;

(3) the project shall not deny any right or benefit, including the right of access to participate in any program of general welfare or the right of access to health care, as a consequence of any individual's decision not to accept family planning services;

(4) the project shall provide family planning acceptors comprehensible information on the health benefits and risks of the method chosen, including those conditions that might render the use of the method inadvisable and those adverse side effects known to be consequent to the use of the method; and

(5) the project shall ensure that experimental contraceptive drugs and devices and medical procedures are provided only in the context of a scientific study in which participants are advised of potential risks and benefits; and, not less than 60 days after the date on which the Administrator of the United States Agency for International Development determines that there has been a violation of the requirements contained in paragraph (1), (2), (3), or (5) of this proviso, or a pattern or practice of violations of the requirements contained in paragraph (4) of this proviso, the Administrator shall submit to the Committees on Appropriations a report containing a description of such violation and the corrective action taken by the Agency.[42]

Representative Tiahrt introduced the amendment amid media and NGO reports that some governments were offering financial incentives to meet sterilization quotas. At that time, many poor women living in rural Peru were reportedly forcibly sterilized and provided with little or no information about alternative contraception methods. In some cases, complications from unsanitary sterilizations led to sickness or death.[43] The intent of the amendment was to ensure that U.S. foreign assistance did not support such practices.[44]

In April 1999, USAID issued guidance on implementing the Tiahrt requirements for voluntary family planning projects. It also provided technical guidance on the "Comprehensible Information" paragraph of the amendment.[45] Since the Tiahrt amendment was enacted, USAID reports there have been violations in Peru, Guatemala, and the Philippines. In 2007, the USAID Inspector General conducted an audit of USAID's compliance with the amendment. Several USAID operating units were audited, including the Global Health Bureau, USAID/Bolivia, USAID/Ethiopia, and USAID/Mali. The audit report, published in February 2008, found no further violations of the amendment.[46]

Most recently, the Tiahrt amendment was included in the FY2012 State-Foreign Operations Appropriations Act. It is applied to family planning assistance funded through all accounts under that act.

EXECUTIVE BRANCH POLICIES AND RESTRICTIONS

This section provides an overview of two executive branch policies addressing abortion or voluntary family planning: the Mexico City policy and USAID Policy Determination 3 (PD-3) on voluntary sterilization.

Mexico City Policy

The Mexico City policy restricted U.S. family planning assistance to foreign NGOs engaged in voluntary abortion activities, even if such activities were conducted with non-U.S. funds. Though the policy was rescinded by the Obama Administration in January 2009, it has remained a controversial issue in U.S. foreign assistance. Unlike the policies listed in the previous section, which were enacted through legislation, the Mexico City policy has been established and rescinded through executive statements and instruments by past and current Presidents.[47]

Reagan through George W. Bush Administrations

At the 1984 International Conference on Population held in Mexico City, the Reagan Administration announced that it would restrict U.S. population assistance by terminating USAID support for any foreign organization—but not national government—that was involved in voluntary abortion activities, even if such activities were undertaken with non-U.S. funds.

The Mexico City policy represented a shift in U.S. population policy. Under the Helms amendment and other abortion and family planning-related restrictions, no U.S. funds could be used directly to pay for the performance of an abortion as a method of family planning or for involuntary sterilizations. However, U.S. and foreign recipients of USAID grants could use their own funds and funds received from other sources to engage, where legal, in abortion-related activities—though they were required to maintain segregated accounts for U.S. money in order to demonstrate compliance with the abortion restrictions. Under the Mexico City policy, foreign NGOs were required to certify in writing that they did not, and would not during the time of the funding agreement, perform or actively promote abortion as a method of family planning as a condition for receiving USAID family planning assistance.

During the George H. W. Bush Administration, several Members of Congress attempted unsuccessfully to overturn the Mexico City policy, arguing that existing congressional restrictions, such as the Helms and Biden amendments, were sufficient. President Clinton, in a January 22, 1993, memo to USAID, lifted restrictions imposed by the Reagan and George H. W. Bush Administrations on grants to family planning NGOs—in effect ending the Mexico City policy. On January 22, 2001, however, President George W. Bush revoked the Clinton Administration memorandum and restored the Mexico City restrictions for the next eight years. He also directed that the restrictions be expanded to State Department programs in the same way they applied to USAID activities. In addition, he clarified that the Mexico City policy did not prohibit the use of U.S. family planning assistance toward post-abortion care.[48]

Obama Administration Rescinds Mexico City Policy

On January 23, 2009, President Obama issued a presidential memorandum to the USAID Administrator and Secretary of State rescinding the Mexico City policy and Bush Administration conditions placed on USAID and the State Department for voluntary population planning activities. The memorandum stated:

> These excessively broad conditions on grants and assistance awards are unwarranted. Moreover, they have undermined efforts to promote safe and effective voluntary family planning programs in foreign nations.[49]

President Obama also directed the Secretary of State and USAID Administrator to waive the conditions set forth by previous Administrations in these policies and to notify current grantees as soon as possible. He further directed the State Department and USAID to cease imposing such conditions on any future grants.

Though the Mexico City policy was rescinded by the Obama Administration, it remains a controversial issue among many Members of Congress. It will likely be an area of continued interest for the 113th Congress and beyond.

USAID Policy Determination 3 on Voluntary Sterilization

Policy Determination 3 (PD-3) on voluntary sterilization (VS) was issued by USAID in September 1982 with the purpose of ensuring that voluntary sterilization services funded by the U.S. government protect the needs and rights of individuals.[50] According to USAID, such protections are necessary given the special nature of VS as a highly personal and permanent surgical procedure.[51] PD-3 outlines a number of requirements for USAID voluntary sterilization services, including the following:

- **Informed consent**—USAID assistance to VS service programs is contingent on satisfactory determination that such services, performed in whole or in part with USAID funds, are performed only after the acceptor of the procedure has voluntarily presented himself or herself at the treatment facility and given his or her informed consent.
- **Ready access to other methods**—Where VS services are available, other means of family planning should also be readily available at a common location, thus allowing the acceptor to have a choice of family planning methods.
- **No incentive payments**—USAID funds cannot be used to pay potential acceptors of sterilization to induce their acceptance of VS. In addition, the fee or cost structure applied to VS and other contraceptives shall be established in such a way that no financial incentive is created for sterilization over another method.[52]

PD-3 also provides guidance on payments to VS service acceptors, providers, and referral agents. Certain types of payment are not considered incentives provided they are "reasonable." Determination of a reasonable payment must be based on a country and program specific basis using knowledge of social and economic circumstances. Specifically:

- **VS acceptors** may generally receive recompense for legitimate extra expenses related to VS (such as transportation, food, medicines, and lost wages during a recovery period);
- **VS service providers** may receive per-case payment and compensation for related items (such as anesthesia, personal costs, transportation, and pre- and post-operative care); and
- **VS service referral agents** may receive per-case payment for extra-expenses incurred in informing or referring VS clients.[53]

PD-3 applies to family planning assistance from any account where USAID funds are used for whole or partial direct support of the performance of voluntary sterilization activities. It applies to U.S. NGOs, foreign NGOs, public international organizations, and governments.

End Notes

[1] 410 U.S. 113 (1973).

[2] The Mexico City policy, which was named after the city where it was introduced, was first announced by President Ronald Reagan at the International Conference on Population held in Mexico in 1984. For more information, see the "Executive Branch Policies and Restrictions" section.

[3] For more information on U.S. policy regarding abortion and family planning domestically and in military medical facilities, see CRS Report 95-724, *Abortion Law Development: A Brief Overview*, by Jon O. Shimabukuro; CRS ReportRL33467, *Abortion: Judicial History and Legislative Response*, by Jon O. Shimabukuro; and CRS Report 95-387, *Abortion Services and Military Medical Facilities*, by David F. Burrelli.

[4] P.L. 87-195; 22 U.S.C. 2151 et seq.

[5] International family planning and abortion-related provisions can also be enacted as part of supplemental appropriations. For more information on foreign aid, see CRS Report R40213, *Foreign Aid: An Introduction to U.S. Programs and Policy*, by Curt Tarnoff and Marian Leonardo Lawson, and CRS Report R40089, *Foreign Assistance Act of 1961: Authorizations and Corresponding Appropriations*, by Dianne E. Rennack and Susan G. Chesser.

[6] The Senate's FY2012 State-Foreign Operations Appropriations Committee Report alludes to this possibility: "The Committee does not continue to carry a general provision specifically regarding funding for abortions and involuntary sterilization (section 7018 of P.L. 111-117), as all but the last sentence of that provision was restatement of permanent law (section 104(f) of the FAA)." U.S. Congress, Senate Committee on Appropriations, *Department of State, Foreign Operations, and Related Programs Appropriations Bill, 2012*, report to accompany S. 1601, 112th Cong., 1st sess., September 22, 2011, S.Rept. 112-85 (Washington: GPO, 2011), p. 32. Similar language was included in the Senate'sFY2011 Foreign Operations Appropriations Committee Report (S.Rept. 111-237, p. 36).

[7] The Department of State, Foreign Operations, and Related Programs Appropriations Act, 2012, is included in Division I of the Consolidated Appropriations Act, 2012 (P.L. 112-74), December 23, 2011.

[8] Section 104(f)(1) of the Foreign Assistance Act of 1961 (P.L. 87-195; 22 U.S.C. 2151b(f)(1)), as amended by the Foreign Assistance Act of 1973 (P.L. 93-189), approved December 17, 1973. "This part" refers to part I of the FAA. For clarification of the term "motivate" in the Helms amendment, see the "Leahy Amendment (1994)" section.

[9] For instance, it was not included in foreign operations appropriations from FY1981 through FY1985. It was included in FY1986 through FY2012 appropriations.

[10] Division I of the Consolidated Appropriations Act, 2012 (P.L. 112-74), approved December 23, 2011.

[11] 125 Stat. 1202.

[12] 125 Stat. 1176.

[13] Section 104(f)(2) of the Foreign Assistance Act of 1961 (P.L. 87-195; 22 U.S.C. 2151b(f)(2)), as amended by Section 104 of the International Development and Food Assistance Act of

1978 (P.L. 95-424; 92 Stat. 946), approved October 6, 1978. "This part" refers to part I of the FAA.

[14] 125 Stat. 1202.

[15] 125 Stat. 1181 -1182.

[16] The provision first appeared under Title III of the Foreign Assistance and Related Programs Appropriations Act, 1979 (P.L. 95-481; 92 Stat. 1597), approved October 18, 1978. For information the circumstances of the amendment's introduction, see, for example, Senate debate, *Congressional Record*, September 22, 1978, Vol. 124, Part 23, pp. S15802-S15804.

[17] *MS 263 Volunteer Pregnancy*, Peace Corps Office of Medical Services (OMS), at http://www.peacecorps.gov/multimedia/pdf/manual/200_Volunteers/260-269_Trainee_and_Volunteer_Medical_Support/MS_263/ Volunteer_Pregnancy.pdf.

[18] Section 104(f)(3) of the Foreign Assistance Act of 1961 (P.L. 87-195; 22 U.S.C. 2151b(f)(3)), as amended by Section 302(b) of the International Security and Development Act of 1981 (P.L. 97-113; 95 Stat. 1532), approved December 29, 1981. "This part" refers to part I of the FAA.

[19] 125 Stat. 1202.

[20] Section 525 of the Foreign Assistance and Related Programs Appropriations Act, 1982 (P.L. 97-121; 95 Stat. 1657), approved December 29, 1981. Representative Siljander's proposed amendment, H.Amdt. 470 to H.R. 4559 [97th], the Foreign Assistance and Related Programs Appropriations Act, 1982, also stated that no U.S. funds would be used to "recommend abortion or to train any individual to perform abortion." This additional language was eliminated in the final bill.

[21] The amendment did not appear in foreign operations appropriations acts for fiscal years 1994 and 1995.

[22] 125 Stat. 1176.

[23] Section 541 of the Foreign Assistance and Related Programs Appropriations Act, 1986 (Section 101(i) of H.J.Res. 465; P.L. 99-190; 99 Stat. 1295), approved December 19, 1985.

[24] John Felton, "Budget Cuts Leave Mark on Foreign Arms Aid," *Congressional Quarterly (CQ) Weekly*, December 21, 1985. Then-USAID Administrator M. Peter McPherson reportedly agreed to provide $40 million over five years to organizations that provide advice such natural methods.

[25] FY2012 State-Foreign Operations Appropriation Act (125 Stat. 1176).

[26] Ibid.

[27] Section 541 of Section 101(i) of H.J.Res. 465, P.L. 99-190 (99 Stat. 1291), approved December 19, 1985.

[28] FY2012 State-Foreign Operations Appropriation Act (125 Stat. 1202-1203).

[29] Ibid.

[30] Chapter V of P.L. 99-88 (99 Stat. 323), approved August 15, 1985. Parts of this section are drawn from CRS Report RL33250, *International Family Planning Programs: Issues for Congress*, by Luisa Blanchfield.

[31] S.Amdt. 388 to H.R. 2577 [99th], agreed to on June 20, 1985.

[32] UNFPA, established in 1969, is the world's largest source of population and reproductive health programs and theprincipal unit within the United Nations for global population issues. For more information, see archived CRS ReportRL32703, *The U.N. Population Fund: Background and the U.S. Funding Debate*, by Luisa Blanchfield.

[33] 125 Stat. 1176.

[34] Division H of the Omnibus Appropriations Act, 2009 (P.L. 111-8; 123 Stat. 909), approved March 11, 2009.

[35] Department of State press release, "U.S. Government Support for the United Nations Population Fund (UNFPA)," March 24, 2009.

[36] 125 Stat. 1264.

[37] Title II of Section 101(f) of H.J.Res. 738, P.L. 99-500 (100 Stat. 1783-217), approved October 18, 1986.

[38] 125 Stat. 1177.

[39] P.L. 103-306 (108 Stat. 1612), approved on August 23, 1994.

[40] FY2012 State-Foreign Operations Appropriations Act (125 Stat. 1177).

[41] Section 101 of the Omnibus Consolidated and Emergency Supplemental Appropriations Act, 1999 (P.L. 105-277, 112 Stat. 2681-154), approved on October 21, 1998.

[42] FY2012 State-Foreign Operations Appropriations Act (125 Stat. 1176-1177). The quotation is formatted for clarity; it appears differently in the act.

[43] Calvin Sims, "Using Gifts as Bait, Peru Sterilizes Poor Women," *New York Times*, February 15, 1998.

[44] For further information on the intent of the Tiahrt amendment and the debate surrounding its adoption, see "Foreign Operations, Export Financing, and Related Programs Appropriations Act, 1999," House debate, *Congressional Record*, Vol. 144, No. 124, September 17, 1998, pp. H7946-H8013.

[45] See (1) *Guidance for Implementing the Tiahrt Requirements for Voluntary Family Planning Projects, USAID*, April 1999, at http://www.usaid.gov/our_work/global_health/pop/tiahrtqa.pdf; and (2) *Technical Guidance on the "Comprehensible Information" Paragraph of the Tiahrt Clause*, USAID, April 1999, at http://www.usaid.gov/our_work/global_health/pop/tiajim3b.pdf.

[46] *Office of the Inspector General: Audit of USAID's Effectiveness in Complying with Tiahrt Voluntary Family Planning* Requirements, Audit Report No. 9-000-08-005-P, February 8, 2008, at http://www.usaid.gov/oig/public/ fy08rpts/9-000-08-005-p.pdf.

[47] For more information on the Mexico City policy, see CRS Report RL33250, *International Family Planning Programs: Issues for Congress*, by Luisa Blanchfield.

[48] White House, "Memorandum for the Administrator of the United States Agency for International Development, Subject: Restoration of the Mexico City Policy," January 22, 2001.

[49] Memorandum from President Obama to the Secretary of State and Administrator for USAID, "Mexico City Policy and Assistance for Voluntary Population Planning," January 23, 2009.

[50] Section V, "Annex" of *Population Assistance—USAID Policy Paper*, USAID Bureau for Program and Policy Coordination, September 1982. Also see *Policy Determination 3 and Addendum: USAID Policy Guidelines on Voluntary Sterilization*.

[51] USAID states that voluntary sterilization services include activities that are primarily intended to provide voluntary male and female sterilizations to persons requesting this type of contraceptive procedure. In the context of PD-3, they may also include voluntary sterilization training programs.

[52] Drawn from *Policy Determination 3 and Addendum: USAID Policy Guidelines on Voluntary Sterilization*. Other requirements are (1) *quality of VS services*: medical personnel who operate on sterilization patients must be well-trained and qualified in accordance with local medical standards, and equipment will be the best available; (2) *sterilization and health services*: VS programs shall be conducted as an integral part of the total health care services of the recipient country and shall be performed with respect to the overall health and well-being of the prospective acceptors; and (3) *country policies*: USAID should take appropriate precautions through consultations with host country officials to minimize the prospect of misunderstandings concerning potential VS activities.

[53] Ibid.

In: U.S. Family Planning ... ISBN: 978-1-62618-532-6
Editors: E.A. Rivera and D.R. Murphy

Chapter 2

INTERNATIONAL FAMILY PLANNING PROGRAMS: ISSUES FOR CONGRESS*

Luisa Blanchfield

SUMMARY

Since 1965, the U.S. government has supported international family planning activities based on principles of voluntarism and informed choice that gives participants access to services and information on a broad range of family planning methods. U.S. family planning policy and abortion restrictions have generated contentious debate for over three decades, resulting in frequent clarification and modification of U.S. international family planning programs. Given the divisive nature of this debate, U.S. funding of these programs will likely remain a point of contention during the 112th Congress.

In 1984, controversy arose over U.S. family planning assistance when the Ronald Reagan Administration introduced restrictions that became known as the "Mexico City policy." The Mexico City policy required foreign non-governmental organizations (NGOs) to certify that they would not perform or actively promote abortion as a method of family planning—even if the activities were undertaken with non-U.S. funds. Presidents Reagan and George H. W. Bush also suspended grants to the U.N. Population Fund (UNFPA) due to evidence of coercive family planning practices in China, citing violations of

* This is an edited, reformatted and augmented version of the Congressional Research Service Publication, CRS Report for Congress RL33250, dated June 26, 2012.

the "Kemp-Kasten" amendment, which bans U.S. assistance to organizations that, as determined by the President, support or participate in the management of coercive family planning programs.

President Bill Clinton resumed UNFPA funding and rescinded the Mexico City policy in 1993. In 2001, however, President George W. Bush reapplied the Mexico City policy restrictions. The Bush Administration also suspended U.S. contributions to UNFPA from FY2002 to FY2008 following a State Department investigation of family planning programs in China. In January 2009, President Barack Obama issued a memorandum rescinding the Mexico City policy. The President also stated that the United States would resume U.S. contributions to UNFPA.

Recent international family planning-related appropriations and Obama Administration requests are outlined below.

- **FY2013**—In February 2012, President Obama requested a total of **$642.7 million** in international family planning and reproductive health (FP/RH) funding, including **$39 million** for UNFPA.
- **FY2012**—In December 2011, President Obama signed the Consolidated Appropriations Act, 2012 (P.L. 112-74), which directs that not less than **$575 million** should be made available for FP/RH activities. It also states that **$35 million** shall be made available for UNFPA.
- **FY2011**—FY2011 appropriations for international family planning and reproductive health are included in the Department of Defense and Full-Year Continuing Appropriations Act, 2011 (P.L. 112-10), which directs that not less that **$575 million** should be made available for international FP/RH activities. It also allocated **$40 million** for UNFPA.

SETTING THE CONTEXT

Population assistance became a global issue in the late 1950s and early 1960s after several private foundations, among them the International Planned Parenthood Federation (IPPF), began providing money to developing countries to address high population growth rates. In 1966, when global population growth rates were reaching an historic annual high of 2.1%, the United Nations began to include population technical assistance in its international development aid programs. Population assistance grew rapidly over the next half-dozen years, with the United States, other developed countries, and international organizations such as the World Bank all beginning to contribute funds. With passage of the Foreign Assistance Act of 1961, Congress first authorized research on international family planning and population issues and, in 1965, the U.S. Agency for International Development (USAID) launched a series of population programs. In 1968, Congress specifically funded international family planning assistance activities and USAID began to purchase contraceptives for distribution through its programs in the developing world.

Most Recent Developments: FY2013 U.S. Family Planning and Reproductive Health Funding

- *Administration Request*: The Obama Administration requested a total of $**642.7** million in international family planning and reproductive health (FP/RH) funding, including $**39** million for the U.N. Population Fund (UNFPA).
- *Senate Actions*: The Senate Committee on Appropriations reported S. 3241 on May 24, 2012, which appropriated a total of $**655.5** million for family planning and reproductive health activities, and $**44.5** million for UNFPA.
- *House Actions*: On May 25, 2012, the House of Representatives Committee on Appropriations reported H.R. 5857, which appropriated not more than $**461** million for family planning and reproductive health activities, and no funds for UNFPA. The House bill also included language that codified the Mexico City Policy.

For more details, see the "U.S. Funding Levels" section.

The first International Population Conference was held in 1974, followed by the second in Mexico City in 1984, and the third in Cairo in 1994.[1] The attention and funding given to international family planning programs are credited with helping to decrease population growth in developing countries from about a 1.7% per year average between 1980 and 2002, to a projected annual average of 1.2% between 2002 and 2015. Nevertheless, while global population growth has slowed, the world's population reached 6 billion in 1999, 6.5 billion in 2005, and 6.9 billion in 2010.[2] It is expected to surpass 9 billion by 2050, with most of the growth occurring in developing nations.[3] In 1960, 70% of the world's population lived in developing countries, and in

2005 the level had grown to 81%. These countries account for the vast majority of worldwide population growth.[4]

The Population Statistics Debate

Population statistics alone are only part of a larger story. For the past 30 years and more, countries have heatedly debated what the statistics mean. Proponents of active family planning programs have held that high fertility rates and rapid population growth are serious impediments to a country's development. According to this school of thought, people are consumers, and no poor country can increase its standard of living and raise its per capita income while wrestling with the problems of trying to feed and care for a rapidly expanding population. Thus, poor and developing countries should invest in family planning programs as part of their economic development process.

On the opposing side, critics of active population planning programs hold that there is little or no correlation between rapid population growth and a country's economic development. Some argue that increased numbers of people provide added productive capacity; therefore, they say, high population growth rates actually can contribute to a country's ability to increase its standard of living. Proponents of this view argue that, at the very least, current economies of scale and global trading patterns have too many empirical variables and uncertainties to establish a direct correlation between population growth and economic development.

Evolution of U.S. Policy (1974 to 1994)

As the population debate evolved, many countries, including the United States, changed their views. At the 1974 international population conference, the United States and other donor countries asserted that high fertility rates were an impediment to economic development—a point that was rejected by developing countries at the time. In keeping with this view, in 1977 the Carter Administration proposed legislative language, later enacted in Section 104(d) of the Foreign Assistance Act of 1961, as amended, that sought to link population growth and traditional development assistance programs on the grounds that a high population growth rate could have a negative effect on other development objectives.

At the second International Conference on Population in Mexico City in 1984, some participants reversed their positions. Many developing countries had become convinced of the urgent need to manage population growth, while U.S. officials asserted that population growth was not necessarily a negative force in economic development, but was instead a neutral phenomenon. At Mexico City, Reagan Administration officials emphasized instead the need for developing countries to adopt sound economic policies that stressed open markets and an active private sector.

Nearly a decade later, the Clinton Administration again changed the U.S. position on family planning programs by lifting U.S. policy announced at the Mexico City Conference. At the 1994 International Conference on Population and Development in Cairo, the U.S. government, along with nearly 200 other nations, endorsed the Conference's program of action, which emphasized a broader population and development agenda, including support for family planning and reproductive health services, improving the status of women, and providing access to safe abortion, where legal.

Trends in Population Approaches and Research

Since the 1994 Cairo conference, groups supporting strategies to address reproductive health and rights have supported a broader agenda of initiatives that includes the promotion of gender equality, increasing adolescent education on sexuality and reproductive health, and ensuring the universal right of health care, including reproductive health. Although endorsed at the July 1999 U.N. meeting of 179 nations to assess progress of the Cairo population conference recommendations, the issues of child education and government responsibilities for ensuring access to safe abortions in countries where the practice is legal were particularly controversial. Some governments opposed the broadening of the Cairo mandate and some, including Argentina, Nicaragua, and the Vatican, filed reservations to the recommendations reached by consensus.

Recent trends in population research indicate that fertility rates in both developed and developing countries have decreased over time. The number of developing countries with high fertility rates (defined as five or more children per woman) declined from 59 in 1990-1995 to 27 in 20052010.[5] Birth rates in developing countries are projected to fall from 2.75 children per woman in 2005-2010 to 2.05 in 2045-2050.[6] At the same time, the numbers of children and young people in developing countries are at an unprecedented high (1.7

billion children and 1.1 billion young people). Consequently, many predict that future world population growth will occur primarily in these countries.[7] Fertility rates in developed countries have been at below-replacement levels for several decades (less than 2.1 children per woman). In recent years, rates have risen slightly; 42 developed nations had below-replacement fertility in 1990-1995, whereas 44 had such levels in 2005-2010. Nevertheless, 25 developed countries—including Japan and the majority of countries in Southern and Eastern Europe—had fertility rates below 1.5 children per woman during the 2005-2010 period.[8]

Although there are differences of opinion as to why fertility rates are falling—and whether the trend is universal throughout the developing world—a few demographers argue that the change has less to do with government family planning policies and foreign aid, and more to do with expanded women's rights in these countries. Women are choosing to have fewer children and have better access to family planning, they argue. Others also contend that with improved economic development, health conditions, and lowered infant mortality rates, parents are deciding to have fewer babies because they are more confident that their children will survive.[9]

Despite projections of declining fertility rates, the world population is expected to increase in the next four decades. If fertility rates continue their decline, many expect the world population to reach about 9.1 billion in 2050, which, according to the median variant, would represent an increase of about 33 million people per year during that period.[10] The exact level of population growth, however, will likely depend on the extent to which individuals—particularly those in developing countries—decide to limit family size and have access to family planning services.[11]

Financing Population Assistance Programs

Financing family planning and basic reproductive health care programs in developing countries became a major issue at the 1994 Cairo population conference. Participating nations agreed that foreign aid donors would provide one-third, or $5.7 billion, of the annual costs of such services, the costs of which were estimated to grow to about $17 billion in 2000. A July 1999 conference assessing implementation of the 1994 Cairo Program of Action, however, found that industrialized countries had fallen far short of the financing goal, providing only about $1.9 billion per year. It also noted that donor allocations still fall far below the targets set at Cairo.[12] A more recent analysis suggests a different trend, noting that donor nations contributed $2.3 billion in 2002, the largest amount ever. In 2008, UNFPA announced that its number of donors had increased from 166 in 2004 to 182 in 2007. In 2009, however, UNFPA reported that the number of its donors decreased to 161; it attributed this decline to the global economic downturn.[13]

Overview of the U.S. Family Planning Debate

Throughout the debate on family planning—at times the most contentious foreign aid issue considered by Congress—the cornerstone of U.S. policy has remained a commitment to funding international family planning programs based on principles of voluntarism and informed choice that give participants access to information and services on a broad range of family planning methods. At present, USAID maintains family planning projects in more than 50 developing countries that include counseling and services, training of health workers, contraceptive commodities and distribution, financial management, policy dialogue, data collection, monitoring and evaluation, public education and marketing, and biomedical and contraceptive research and development. USAID applies a broad reproductive health approach to its family planning programs, increasingly integrating it with other interventions in maternal and child health, the enhancement of the status of women, and HIV prevention. It also supports programs that address behavior change communication, post-abortion care, and obstetric fistula.[14]

In addition to differences of opinion over how population growth affects economic development in developing countries, family planning assistance has become a source of substantial controversy among U.S. policymakers, centering on two key issues: (1) the use of federal funds to perform or promote abortions abroad and how to deal with evidence of coercion in some national family planning programs, especially in China, and (2) setting appropriate and effective funding levels for family planning assistance.

Arguably, the most bitter controversies in U.S. family planning policy have erupted over abortion—in particular, the degree to which legal abortions and coercive programs occur in other countries' family planning programs, the extent to which U.S. funds should be granted to or withheld from such countries and organizations that administer these programs, and the effect that withholding U.S. funds might have on global population growth and access to voluntary family planning services in developing nations. These issues stem from the contentious domestic debate over U.S. domestic abortion policy that has continued since the Supreme Court's 1973 *Roe v. Wade* decision holding that the Constitution protects a woman's decision whether to terminate her pregnancy. In every Congress since 1973, abortion opponents have introduced constitutional amendments or legislation that would prohibit abortions supported with U.S. foreign assistance funds. As an alternative, abortion critics have also persuaded Congress to attach numerous provisions to annual appropriation measures banning the use of federal funds for performing legal abortions.

Much of this debate has focused on domestic spending bills, especially restrictions on abortions under the Medicaid program in the Labor/Health and Human Services appropriation legislation. However, the controversy spilled over into U.S. foreign aid policy almost immediately when Congress approved an amendment to the Foreign Assistance Act of 1961 in late 1973 introduced by then-Senator Jesse Helms (§104(f)). The provision, widely referred to as the "Helms amendment," prohibits the use of foreign development assistance to (1) pay for the performance of abortions or involuntary sterilizations, (2) motivate or coerce any person to practice abortions, or (3) coerce or provide persons with any financial incentive to undergo sterilizations. Since 1981, Congress has enacted nearly identical restrictions in annual Foreign Operations appropriation bills.[15]

For the past several decades, both congressional actions and administration directives have restricted U.S. population assistance in various ways, including those set out in the Foreign Assistance Act of 1961, as well as executive regulations and appropriation provisions prohibiting *indirect* support for coercive family planning (specifically in China) and abortion activities related to the work of international and foreign NGOs. Two issues in particular which were initiated in the mid-1980s—the Mexico City policy involving funding for foreign non-governmental organizations, and restrictions on funding for the U.N. Population Fund (UNFPA) because of its activities in China—have remained controversial and continue as prominent features in the family planning debate.

THE MEXICO CITY POLICY

In 1984, the Reagan Administration announced that it would restrict U.S. population aid by terminating USAID support for any foreign non-governmental organizations (NGOs) (but not national governments) that were involved in voluntary abortion activities, even if such activities were undertaken with non-U.S. funds. U.S. officials presented the revised policy at the 2nd U.N. International Conference on Population in Mexico City in 1984. Thereafter, it become known as the "Mexico City policy." During the George H. W. Bush Administration, efforts were made in Congress to overturn the Mexico City policy and rely on existing congressional restrictions in the Foreign Assistance Act of 1961 banning direct U.S. funding of abortions and coerced sterilizations. Provisions adopted by the House and/or Senate that would have reversed the policy, however, were removed from legislation under threat of a presidential veto.

Critics charge that the Mexico City policy is a violation of free speech and the rights of women to choose to have an abortion in countries where it is legal. They contend that the policy undermines family planning and maternal health care services offered in developing nations and may actually contribute to the rise in the number of abortions performed, including some that are unsafe and illegal. They further emphasize that family planning organizations may cut back on services because they are unsure of the full implications of the restrictions and do not want to risk USAID funding. Opponents also believe that the conditions of the Mexico City policy undermine relations between the U.S. government and foreign NGOs and multilateral groups, creating a situation in which the United States challenges their right to determine how to spend their own money and imposes a so-called gag order on their ability to promote changes to abortion laws and regulations in developing nations. The latter, these critics note, would be unconstitutional if applied to American groups working in the United States.

Mexico City Policy Rescinded by the Bill Clinton Administration (1993)

President Clinton, in a January 22, 1993, memo to USAID, lifted restrictions imposed by the Reagan and Bush Administrations on grants to family planning foreign NGOs—in effect ending the Mexico City policy. The memo noted that the policy had extended beyond restrictions in the Foreign Assistance Act and was not mandated by law. In his remarks, President Clinton explained that this step would "reverse a policy that has seriously undermined much needed efforts to promote safe and effective family planning programs abroad, and will allow us to once again provide leadership in helping to stabilize world population."[16]

The George W. Bush Administration Restores the Mexico City Policy (2001)

On January 22, 2001, President George W. Bush revoked the Clinton Administration memorandum and restored in full the terms of the Mexico City restrictions. In making the announcement, the White House Press Secretary stated that the "President is committed to maintaining the $425 million funding level provided in the FY2001 appropriation because he knows that one of the best ways to prevent abortion is by providing quality voluntary family planning services."[17]

Bush Administration Mexico City Policy Guidelines

On February 15, 2001, USAID released specific guidelines necessary to implement President Bush's directive. The guidelines stated that U.S. NGOs receiving USAID grants could not furnish assistance to foreign NGOs that (1) performed or actively promoted abortion as a method of family planning in USAID-recipient countries, or (2) furnished assistance to other foreign NGOs that conducted such activities. When USAID provided assistance directly to a foreign NGO, the organization had to certify that it did not now or would not during the term of the grant perform or actively promote abortion as a method of family planning or provide financial support to other foreign NGOs that carry out such activities. The implementing regulations contained several exceptions, including the following:

- Abortions could be performed if the life of the mother would be endangered if the fetus were carried to term or following rape or incest; health care facilities may treat injuries or illnesses caused by legal or illegal abortions (post-abortion care).
- "Passive" responses by family planning counselors to questions about abortion from pregnant women who have already decided to have a legal abortion were not considered an act of promoting abortion; referrals for abortion as a result of rape, incest, or where the mother's life would be endangered, or for post-abortion care are permitted.

USAID was able to continue support to foreign governments, either directly or through a grantee, even in cases where the government included abortion in its family planning program. Money provided to such governments, however, had to be placed in a segregated account and none of the funds could be drawn to finance abortion activities.

President Bush issued a memorandum on August 29, 2003, for the Secretary of State, directing that the Mexico City policy conditions be applied to State Department programs in the same way they applied to USAID activities. This directive mostly impacted State Department-managed refugee programs, large portions of which were implemented by international organizations and NGOs. The President's memorandum, however, stated that the policy would not apply to multilateral organizations that were associations of governments, presumably referring to the U.N. High Commissioner for Refugees, among others. President Bush further stated that the Mexico City policy would not apply to foreign aid funds authorized under P.L. 108-25, the United States Leadership Against HIV/AIDS, Tuberculosis, and Malaria Act of 2003.

As was the case during the 1980s and early 1990s when the Mexico City policy was in place, foreign NGOs, as a condition for receipt of U.S. family planning assistance, would need to certify that they would not perform or actively promote abortions as a method of family planning in other countries. President Bush, in announcing the policy change, noted that American taxpayer funds should not be used to pay for abortions or to advocate or actively promote abortion.

Supporters of the certification requirement argue that even though permanent law bans USAID funds from being used to perform abortions, money is fungible; organizations receiving American-taxpayer funding can use USAID resources for family planning activities while diverting money raised from other sources to perform abortions or lobby to change abortion laws and regulations. The certification process, they contend, stops the fungibility "loophole."

Obama Administration Rescinds the Mexico City Policy (2009)

On January 23, 2009, President Barack Obama issued a presidential memorandum to the Secretary of State and USAID Administrator revoking the Mexico City policy and Bush Administration conditions on voluntary population planning provided by the State Department.[18] The memorandum stated:

> These excessively broad conditions on grants and assistance awards are unwarranted. Moreover, they have undermined efforts to promote safe and effective voluntary family planning programs in foreign nations.[19]

President Obama also directed the Secretary of State and USAID Administrator to waive the conditions set forth in these policies and to notify current grantees as soon as possible. He further directed the State Department and USAID to cease imposing such conditions on any future grants.[20]

RESTRICTIONS ON U.N. POPULATION FUND (UNFPA) FUNDING: THE "KEMP-KASTEN AMENDMENT"

At the 1984 Mexico City Conference, the Reagan Administration instituted a new policy relating to UNFPA.[21] The Administration required that the organization provide "concrete assurances that [it] is not engaged in, or does not provide funding for, abortion or coercive family planning programs." It was particularly concerned with UNFPA's activities in China, where, according to Administration officials, there was evidence of coercive family planning practices.

Subsequently, Congress legislated a more restrictive UNFPA policy—believed to be aimed at coercive Chinese family planning programs and UNFPA's continuing operations in the country— by enacting the "Kemp-Kasten amendment" in the FY1985 Supplemental Appropriations Act (P.L. 99-88). The amendment prohibited the use of appropriated funds for any organization or program, as determined by the President, found to be supporting or participating "in the management" of a program of coercive abortion or involuntary sterilization. Following enactment of P.L. 99-88, USAID announced that $10 million of $46 million that had been directed for UNFPA during FY1985 would be redirected to other programs due to concerns regarding UNFPA's activities in China, and later said that the United States would not contribute to UNFPA at all in 1986. Most of the $25 million that was originally allocated for UNFPA was spent on other international family planning activities. Even though this pattern to redirect UNFPA transfers to other population assistance programs continued, critics of the Kemp-Kasten amendment and the President's determination to suspend contributions asserted that UNFPA was the world's most effective family planning organization, and that the quality of services provided in developing nations outside of China suffered due to the unwillingness of the United States to support them. At the time of suspension, U.S. payments represented nearly one-third of UNFPA's annual budget. From 1986 through 1993, no U.S. contributions went to UNFPA.

The Clinton Administration lifted the ban on UNFPA contributions, making available $14.5 million in FY1993 but stipulating that funds could not be used in China. Congressional critics of China's family planning practices attempted unsuccessfully to attach provisions to various foreign aid bills banning U.S. contributions unless UNFPA withdrew from China or the President could certify that China no longer maintained a coercive family planning program. While the United States continued to support UNFPA during the next eight years (except for FY1999), Congress attached restrictions in appropriation measures that in most cases reduced the U.S. contribution by the proportionate share of UNFPA funds spent on China.

George W. Bush Administration Determinations under Kemp-Kasten

For FY2002, Congress provided not more than $34 million for UNFPA. But in mid-January 2002, the Bush Administration placed a hold on U.S. contributions to UNFPA, pending a review of the organization's program in China. The White House said it initiated the review because of new evidence that coercive practices continued in counties where UNFPA concentrated its programs.[22]

From FY2002 through FY2008, the Bush Administration determined that UNFPA was ineligible for U.S. funding under the Kemp-Kasten amendment.[23] Since the 2002 determination, the Administration transferred $34 million from each of FY2002, FY2004, and FY2005 appropriations, and $25 million from FY2003 funds that would have otherwise been provided to UNFPA to support bilateral family planning programs and activities combating human trafficking and prostitution. Approximately $22.5 million in unused UNFPA funds from FY2006 was transferred to the International Organizations and Program (IOP) account.

State Department Team Assesses UNFPA Program in China

While most observers agree that coercive family planning practices continue in China, differences remain over the extent, if any, to which UNFPA is involved in involuntary activities and whether UNFPA should operate at all in a country where such conditions exist. Given conflicting reports, a State Department investigative team visited China in May 2002 and reported a series of findings and recommendations. The team found no evidence that UNFPA "has knowingly supported or participated in the management of a program of coercive abortion or involuntary sterilization" in China, and recommended the United States release not more than $34 million of previously appropriated funds to UNFPA.[24]

Nevertheless, on July 22, 2002, Secretary of State Powell, to whom President Bush had delegated the decision, announced that UNFPA was in violation of Kemp-Kasten and ineligible for U.S. funding. The State Department's analysis of the Secretary's determination found that even though UNFPA did not "knowingly" support or participate in a coercive practice, that alone would not preclude the application of Kemp-Kasten.[25] Instead, a finding that the recipient of U.S. funds—in this case UNFPA—simply supports or participates in such a program, whether knowingly or unknowingly, would trigger the restriction. The assessment team found that the Chinese government imposed fines and penalties on families ("social compensation fees") that have children exceeding the number approved by the government. The department further noted that UNFPA had funded computers and data-processing equipment that had helped strengthen the management of the Chinese State Family Planning Commission. Beyond the legitimate uses of these and other items financed by UNFPA, such equipment facilitated, in the view of the State Department, China's ability to impose social compensation fees or perform coercive abortions. The State Department analysis concluded that UNFPA's involvement in China's family planning program "allows the Chinese government to implement more effectively its program of coercive abortion."

On September 17, 2005, the State Department stated that the United States had been urging UNFPA and China to modify the organization's program in a manner that would permit U.S. support to resume, but that no key changes had occurred that would allow a resumption of U.S. funding under the conditions of the Kemp-Kasten provision. Subsequently, on October 18 of that year, USAID notified Congress that the reprogrammed UNFPA set-aside would be made available to expand family planning and reproductive health programs in 14 other countries.[26]

Bush Administration Response to the New UNFPA China Program

The September 17 announcement followed a June 22, 2005, UNFPA Executive Board meeting to consider UNFPA's new five-year, $27 million program for China. At the meeting, Kelly Ryan, Deputy Assistant Secretary of State for the Bureau of Population, Refugees and Migration, argued that UNFPA should end its operations in China because of the coercive nature of China's family planning programs. Two days later, State Department spokesperson Sean McCormick issued a statement saying the United States was "disappointed" that UNFPA had decided to continue financial and technical support to the Chinese birth limitation program. He noted that U.S. opposition was not aimed at UNFPA but was a "matter of principle," based on strong American opposition to "human rights abuses associated with coercive birth limitation regimes." He acknowledged that UNFPA does not approve of coercive policies but that the organization's continued presence in China offered a "seal of approval" for Chinese policies.

Opposition to the Bush Administration Determination

Critics of the Bush Administration's decision opposed it for a number of reasons. They argued that access to voluntary family planning programs by persons in around 140 countries would be reduced, undermining the health of women and children, increasing unwanted pregnancies, and increasing the likelihood of higher numbers of abortions. Still other critics were concerned about the possible application of the Administration's interpretation of Kemp-Kasten to other international organizations operating in China and to which the United States contributes—for example, UNICEF, WHO, and the U.N. Development Program.

Obama Administration Determinations under Kemp-Kasten

The Obama Administration has expressed its support for U.S. funding of UNFPA. In a January 2009 memorandum rescinding the Mexico City policy, President Obama indicated that his Administration would fund UNFPA. In March 2009, a State Department spokesperson confirmed that the U.S. government would contribute $50 million to UNFPA as provided by the Omnibus Appropriations Act, 2009 (P.L. 111-8). This decision, according to Administration officials, highlights the President's "strong commitment" to international family planning, women's health, and global development.[27]

2011 State Department Human Rights Report on China

The broad question concerning the degree of coercive family planning practices in China remains a controversial matter. The State Department's most recent human rights report on China (covering 2011) concluded that:

"National law prohibits the use of physical coercion to compel persons to submit to abortion or sterilization. However, intense pressure to meet birth limitation targets set by government regulations resulted in instances of local family-planning officials using physical coercion to meet government goals. Such practices included the mandatory use of birth control and the abortion of unauthorized pregnancies.

In the case of families that already had two children, one parent was often pressured to undergo sterilization...

The population control policy relied on education, propaganda, and economic incentives, as well as on more coercive measures. Those who violated the child-limit policy by having an unapproved child or helping another do so faced disciplinary measures such as social compensation fees, job loss or demotion, loss of promotion opportunity, expulsion from the Communist Party of China (membership is an unofficial requirement for certain jobs), and other administrative punishments, including in some cases the destruction of private property."[28]

According to the report, female infanticide, sex-selective abortions, and the abandonment and neglect of baby girls remained a problem due to traditional preferences for sons and the coercive birth limitation policy.[29]

Family Planning Conditions in China

As noted, much of this debate has focused on UNFPA's programs in China, both because of China's well-known population growth and because of widespread publicity given to reports of coercion in its family planning programs. China's population increased from 500 million in 1950 to 1.008 billion according to the 1982 census—an average annual growth rate of 2%, or a doubling of the population every 36 years. (Although the 2% rate is not particularly large by developing country standards, many consider a lower rate crucial to China's economic development prospects given the country's already huge population size.) In 2010, China's estimated population was just over 1.33 billion.[30] Chinese authorities came to view control of population growth not simply as an important priority, but as a necessity for the nation's survival. In an attempt to reach a 1% annual population growth rate, Chinese authorities, in 1979, instituted a policy of allowing only one child per couple, providing monetary bonuses and other benefits as incentives to comply. Women with one living child who became pregnant a second time were said to be subjected to rigorous pressure to end the pregnancy and undergo sterilization; couples who actually had a second child faced heavy fines, employment demotions, and other penalties. Chinese leaders have admitted that coerced abortions and involuntary sterilizations occur, but insist that those involved are acting outside the law and are punished, particularly through the Administrative Procedure Law enacted in October 1990. Chinese authorities have termed female infanticide an "intolerable crime" that must be punished by law. Other press reports suggest that the Chinese State Family Planning Commission (SFPC) has softened some of its previous harsh tactics to limit population growth. A number of counties have ended the system of permits for pregnancy and quotas for the number of children that can be born annually. When it launched in January 1998 a new $20 million, five-year program in China, UNFPA announced that SFPC officials had agreed to drop birth targets in the 32 counties where U.N. activities would be focused. And in May 1999, the city of Beijing ended an eight-year policy that women had to be at least 24 years old to bear a child and lifted the requirement for couples to obtain a certificate before having a child. On September 1, 2002, China adopted the Population and Family Planning Law, the country's first formal law on this subject. The law, which requires couples who have an unapproved child to pay a "social compensation fee" and extends preferential treatment to couples who abide by the birth limits, is intended to standardize the implementation of the government's birth limitation policies. The State Department Country Reports on Human Rights Practices for 2006 (dated March 2007), however, found that enforcement of the law varied by location. Following the May 2002 State Department investigation of Chinese policies, senior department officials began a series of discussions with China regarding its birth planning law. Arthur Dewey, Assistant Secretary of State for Population, Refugees, and Migration, told the House International Relations Committee in December 2004, that in six rounds of talks with Chinese officials, there had been "encouraging movement" in China's approach to population policy and the reduction of coercive practices.[31] Nevertheless, Assistant Secretary Dewey said that the social compensation fee policy set out in China's national law on population and birth planning is a "harsh and effective enforcement tool" that is used to force women to have an abortion, and is therefore regarded as a coercive policy. While negotiations have resulted in some progress, he concluded that China's policies have not been altered enough to allow the Bush Administration to resume UNFPA funding. As noted previously, U.S. officials continued to voice their opposition at a UNFPA Executive Board meeting on June 22, 2005, where members met to consider a new, five-year (2006-2010), $27 million UNFPA program in China. A State Department press release on June 24 again acknowledged that China had made some progress in its approach to population issues, but argued that Beijing's birth limitation policy continues to contain several coercive elements, including the social maintenance fee for unplanned births, and regulations that limit choices by women other than to undergo an abortion. At the June 22 meeting, China's deputy U.N. Ambassador Zhang Yishan argued that due to the size of China's population, it had to maintain a strong family planning program, and that without the policies of the last 30 years, China's population would have grown by 300 million additional people. He countered that, by law, family planning workers are not permitted to utilize coercive measures in their work. The UNFPA Executive Board approved a five-year program for China on January 30, 2006. Prior to the signing, U.S. Deputy Representative to the United Nations, Ambassador Alejandro Wolff, expressed disappointment that no substantive changes had been made to the draft plan that had been reviewed in mid-2005. He argued that UNFPA assistance provided a "de facto United Nations 'seal of approval'" to China's "abhorrent" practices. He further asserted that the new Country Program Document for China was incorrect in its claim that China was committed to implementing the Cairo Population Conference action plan, a program that excluded coercive practices in family planning activities.[32] A group of 10 European nations disagreed, however, issuing a statement saying that China did conform to the program of 1994 International Conference on Population and Development.[33] On August 30, 2010, the UNFPA Executive Board approved a new five-year program for China that spans from 2011 through 2015. The proposed budget for the program is $22 million.[34]

U.S. Funding Levels

Since 1965, USAID has obligated over $13.8 billion in assistance for international family planning. In many years, and especially over the past two decades, the level of funding for population assistance has been controversial, and at times, linked directly with differences concerning Mexico City policy restrictions and abortion. Until FY1996, Congress generally supported higher funding levels for population aid than proposed by the President, especially during the Reagan and Bush Administrations. During the balance of the Clinton Administration, however, Congress cut and placed restrictions on bilateral funding (see **Table 1**). In some years, bilateral family planning, reproductive health, and maternal health levels received additional resources when UNFPA-earmarked funds were reprogrammed for bilateral activities after UNFPA was determined to be ineligible for U.S. support under the Kemp-Kasten amendment. In FY2009, total U.S. population assistance was approximately $572.4 million, an increase of about $115 million over the FY2008 level of $457.2 million. U.S. population assistance levels peaked in FY2010, with USAID estimating that total assistance, including contributions to UNFPA, reached a high $648.4 million.[35] This increase in funding can be attributed in part to President Obama's determination that UNFPA is eligible for U.S. funding under the Kemp-Kasten amendment and to the President's Global Health Initiative (GHI).

FY2013 Administration Request and Congressional Actions

In February 2012, President Obama requested a total of $642.7 million for FY2013 international family planning and reproductive health funding.[36] This includes $530 million from the Global Health Programs account (GHP, formerly Global Health and Child Survival), $73.7 million from the Economic Support Fund (ESF), and $39 million for UNFPA from the International Organizations and Programs account (IO&P). The Senate Committee on Appropriations reported S. 3241, the Department of State, Foreign Operations, and Related Programs Appropriations Act, 2013, on May 24, 2012. The bill appropriated a total of $655.5 million for family planning and reproductive health activities, and $44.5 million for UNFPA.[37] On May 25, 2012, the House of Representatives reported H.R. 5857, the Department of State, Foreign Operations, and Related Programs Appropriations Act, 2013. It appropriated not more than $461 million in reproductive health and voluntary family planning funding, and no funds for UNFPA. The House bill also included language in Section 7056 that codified the Mexico City Policy.[38]

Table 1. U.S. Family Planning Assistance, FY1995-FY2012
(Family planning/reproductive health budget; millions of current $)

	1995	1996	1997	1998	1999	2000	2001	2002[c]	2003[c]	2004[c]	2005[c]	2006[c]	2007[c]	2008[c]	2009	2010	2011	2012
Bilateral Aid	542.0	432.0	385.0	385.0	385.0	372.0[a]	425.0	425.0	443.6	429.5	437.0	435.0	435.6	457.2	522.4	593.4	575.0	575.0
UNFPA	35.0	22.8	25.0	20.0	0.0	21.5[b]	21.5[b]	0.0	0.0	0.0	0.0	0.0	0.0	0.0	50.0	55.0	40.0	35.0
Total	577.0	454.8	410.0	405.0	385.0	393.5	446.5	425.0	443.6	429.5	437.0	435.0	435.6	457.2	572.4	648.4[d]	615.0[e]	610.0[e]

Source: USAID Bureau of Global Health Strategic Planning and Budgeting Office and annual appropriations legislation.

Note: Amounts are adjusted for rescissions in appropriate years.

a. The bilateral FY2000 aid level reflects a transfer of $12.5 million from population assistance to child survival activities.

b. UNFPA amounts for FY2000 and FY2001 reflect a $3.5 million deduction due to legislative restrictions.

c. From FY2002 through FY2008, the Bush Administration determined that UNFPA was ineligible for U.S. funding because of its programs in China, and withheld appropriated funds. Some of the withheld funds were reallocated for USAID bilateral family planning, vulnerable children, and counter-trafficking in persons programs.

d. This figure is an estimate.

e. These figures represent the enacted level.

FY2012 Appropriations and Administration Request

On December 23, 2011, President Obama signed the Consolidated Appropriations Act, 2012 (P.L. 112-74), which directs that not less than $575 million should be made available for family planning and reproductive health activities. The act also states that $35 million shall be made available for UNFPA. As during previous appropriations cycles, UNFPA funding is subject to certain restrictions, including:

- none of the funds made available may be used by UNFPA for a country program in China;
- U.S. contributions must be kept in an account separate from other UNFPA accounts and should not commingle with other sums; and
- UNFPA must not fund abortions.

In addition, four months after the enactment of P.L. 112-74, the Secretary of State is required to report to the Committees on Appropriations on the funds that UNFPA is budgeting for that year for its country program in China. The act also specifies that any funds not made available to UNFPA because of any provision of law shall be transferred to the Global Health Programs account and shall be made available for family planning, maternal, and reproductive health activities.

For FY2012, the Obama Administration requested a total of $769.105 million for international family planning and reproductive health assistance. This included $625.6 million from the Global Health and Child Survival account (GHCS); $89.073 million from ESF; and $6.932 million from the Assistance to Europe, Eurasia, and Central Asia account (AEECA). In addition, it requested $47.5 million for UNFPA through the IO&P account.

FY2011 Appropriations and Administration Request

FY2011 appropriations for international family planning and reproductive health are stated in the Department of Defense and Full-Year Continuing Appropriations Act, 2011 (P.L. 112-10).[39] The act directs that not less that $575 million should be made available for international family planning and reproductive health activities.[40] It also states that not less than $40 million should be directed to UNFPA, to be drawn from the IO&P account, and maintains the same UNFPA restrictions included in FY2010 appropriations (P.L. 111-117, see below).[41]

In March 2010, President Obama requested a total of $715.74 million for bilateral and multilateral family planning and reproductive health assistance. This included $590 million from GHCS, $65.267 million from ESF, and $10.473 million from AEECA. It also requested $50 million for UNFPA to be funded through the IO&P account.[42]

FY2010 Appropriations and Administration Request

On December 16, 2009, President Obama signed the Consolidated Appropriations Act, 2010 (P.L. 111-117). Division F of that bill, the Department of State, Foreign Operations, and Related Programs Appropriations Act, 2010, directs that not less than $648.457 million should be made available for international family planning and reproductive health activities. Of this amount, $525 million shall be made available under the USAID GHCS account, and $55 million shall be made available for UNFPA under the IO&P account. The remaining amounts will be made available under other accounts, including $58.849 million from ESF, and $9.608 million from AEECA.

Section 7078 of P.L. 111-117 outlines funding restrictions for UNFPA. As stated above, it allocates $55 million for UNFPA to be made available under IO&P. The bill also establishes a number of conditions for U.S. contributions to UNFPA. Specifically, none of the funds made available may be used by UNFPA for a country program in China. In addition:

- U.S. contributions to UNFPA must be kept in an account separate from other accounts at UNFPA and should not commingle with other sums; and
- for UNFPA to receive U.S. funding, it must not fund abortions;

The bill also establishes related reporting requirements for the Secretary of State. Not later than four months after the enactment of P.L. 111-117, the Secretary was required to submit a report to the Committees on Appropriations indicating the funds UNFPA is budgeting for a country program in China. If the Secretary's report indicates that funds will be spent on such a program, then the amount of such funds shall be deducted from the funds made available to UNFPA for the remainder of the fiscal year in which the report is submitted.[43]

The Obama Administration had requested a total of $593.457 million for international family planning and reproductive health activities in FY2010. This included $475 million from the USAID GHCS account, $58.849 million from ESF, and $9.608 million from AEECA. The Administration also requested $50 million for UNFPA funding to be made available under the IO&P account.[44]

End Notes

[1] The conferences were coordinated by the United Nations. More information is available at http://www.un.org/esa/devagenda/population.html.

[2] Overview and highlights of the Population Reference Bureau (PRB) *2010 World Population Data Sheet*, athttp://www.prb.org/Publications/Datasheets/2010/2010wpds.aspx.

[3] *2008 Revision of World Population Prospects,* U.N. Statistics Division, March 11, 2009.

[4] PRB, *Frequently Asked Questions About the PRB World Population Data Sheet*, 2005.

[5] *2008 Revision of World Population Prospects, Key Findings,* U.N. Statistics Division, March 11, 2009.

[6] "Linking Population, Poverty, and Development: Rapid Growth in Less Developed Regions," U.N. Population Fund, 2010.

[7] PRB, *2010 World Population Data Sheet*, p. 3.

[8] *2008 Revision of World Population Prospects, Key Findings,* U.N. Statistics Division, March 11, 2009.

[9] World Bank, "Population Growth Rate," at http://www.worldbank.org/depweb/english/modules/social/pgr/.

[10] *2008 Revision of World Population Prospects, Key Findings,* U.N. Statistics Division, March 11, 2009.

[11] PRB, *2010 World Population Data Sheet*, p. 3.

[12] Population Action International, *Progress and Promises: Trends in International Assistance for Reproductive Health and Population* 2004.

[13] See (1) *UNFPA 2007 Annual Report*, U.N. Population Fund, 2008; (2) U.N. document, DP/FPA/2010/18, dated April 30, 2010; and (3) *UNFPA 2009 Annual Report*, U.N. Population Fund, 2010.

[14] For further information on USAID family planning and reproductive health programs, see http://www.usaid.gov/our_work/global_health/pop/index.html.

[15] For more information on the Helms amendment and other abortion and family planning-related restrictions, see CRS Report R41360, *Abortion and Family Planning-Related Provisions in U.S. Foreign Assistance Law and Policy*, by Luisa Blanchfield

[16] President Bill Clinton, "Remarks on Signing Memorandums on Medical Research and Reproductive Health and an Exchange With Reporters," January 22, 1993.

[17] The White House. Office of the Secretary. *Restoration of the Mexico City Policy,* January 22, 2001.

[18] Specifically, President Obama's memorandum revoked President Bush's January 22, 2001, memorandum for the USAID Administrator (Restoration of the Mexico City Policy) and the August 29, 2003, memorandum for the Secretary of State (Assistance for Voluntary Population Planning).

[19] Memorandum from President Obama to the Secretary of State and Administrator for USAID, "Mexico City Policy and Assistance for Voluntary Population Planning," January 23, 2009, available at http://www.whitehouse.gov/the_press_office/MexicoCityPolicy-Voluntary PopulationPlanning/.

[20] Ibid.

[21] UNFPA is a U.N. specialized agency that "supports countries in using population data for policies and programs" to improve reproductive health, prevent HIV/AIDS, promote gender equality, and make motherhood safer. UNFPA was the lead U.N. agency for the 1994 International Conference on Population and Development in Cairo. For more detailed information regarding UNFPA, see CRS Report RL32703, *The U.N. Population Fund: Background and the U.S. Funding Debate*, by Luisa Blanchfield.

[22] See House International Relations Committee hearing, *Coercive Population Control in China: New Evidence of Forced Abortion and Forced Sterilization*, October 17, 2001, and a Senate Foreign Relations Committee hearing, *U.S. Funding for the U.N. Population Fund: The Effect on Women's Lives*, February 27, 2002.

[23] For the most recent Administration statements, see "White House: No U.N. Funding for China," *The Associated Press,* September 7, 2007, and Press statement by Tom Casey, Deputy Spokesman, "Fiscal Year 2008 Funding for the United Nations Population Fund (UNFPA)," U.S. Department of State, June 27, 2008, available at http://www.state.gov/r/pa/prs/ps/2008/jun/106348.htm.

[24] See http://www.state.gov/g/prm/rls/rpt/2002/12122.htm for report's full text.

[25] See http://www.state.gov/g/prm/rls/other/12128.htm for a full text of the determination.

[26] The most significant increases were made in programs for Georgia, Madagascar, Romania, Russia, Rwanda, and Ukraine.

[27] Department of State press release, "U.S. Government Support for the United Nations Population Fund (UNFPA)," March 24, 2009.

[28] "Country Reports on Human Rights Practices, 2011—China," U.S. Department of State, Bureau of Democracy, Human Rights and Labor, April 8, 2011, available at http://www.state.gov/j/drl/rls/hrrpt/humanrightsreport/index.htm#wrapper.

[29] Ibid.

[30] Central Intelligence Agency, The World Factbook, China. For earlier data, see The World Bank, "China—Data," at http://data.worldbank.org/country/china.

[31] Dewey cited, for example, the elimination of a requirement for married couples to obtain government permission prior to pregnancy in 25 of China's 31 provinces, municipalities, and autonomous regions. He also noted the government's launch of a public information project highlighting the status of the girl child. He viewed this as a positive step towards ending discrimination in China against girls and women.

[32] U.S. Mission to the United Nations. *Ambassador Wolff: Remarks on Proposed UNFPA Sixth Country Program for China,* January 26, 2006.

[33] "UN Population Fund Endorses 27-million-dollar China Program," *Agence France Presse*, January 30, 2006.

[34] U.N. document, DP/FPA/CPD/CHN/7, *United Nations Population Fund Final Country Program Document for China,* dated July 16, 2010.

[35] Department of State press release, "U.S. Government Support for the United Nations Population Fund (UNFPA)," March 24, 2009.

[36] Congressional Budget Justification, Volume 2, Foreign Operations, Department of State, February 2012, p. 314.

[37] U.S. Congress, Senate Committee on Appropriations, *Department of State, Foreign Operations, and Related Programs Appropriations Bill, 2013*, report to accompany S. 3241, 112th Cong., 2nd sess., May 24, 2012, S.Rept. 112-172 (Washington: GPO, 2012), pp. 40-41. Of the $655.5 million, $600 million shall be drawn from the GHP account and $55.5 million from ESF.

[38] U.S. Congress, House Committee on Appropriations, *State, Foreign Operations, and Related Programs Appropriations Bill, 2013*, report to accompany H.R. 5857, 112th Cong., 2nd sess., May 25, 2012, H.Rept. 112-494 (Washington: GPO, 2012), pp. 35, 70.

[39] Congress did not enact legislation to fund foreign operations programs for FY2011. Instead, §1101(a)(6) of P.L. 112-10 continues the Consolidated Appropriations Act, 2010 (P.L. 111-117) to fund FY2011.

[40] When addressing FY2011 U.S. assistance for reproductive health and family planning, §2120(e) of P.L. 112-10 refers to and substitutes language from §7060 of Division F of P.L. 111-117, which directed not less than $648,457,000 for family planning and reproductive health. (Specifically, P.L. 112-10 says that $575,000,000 shall be substituted for $648,457,000.)

[41] When addressing FY2011 UNFPA funding, §2120(e) of P.L. 112-10 refers to and substitutes language from §660(a) of Division J of P.L. 110-161, the Consolidated Appropriations Act, 2008, which states that not less than $7 million shall be derived from funds appropriated under the IO&P heading. (Specifically, P.L. 112-10 substitutes "$40,000,000 should" for "not less than $7,000,000 shall.")

[42] Congressional Budget Justification, Foreign Operations, FY2011, Volume 2, U.S. Department of State, p. 240.

[43] See §7078(e)(1), (2).

[44] Congressional Budget Justification, Foreign Operations, FY2010, U.S. Department of State, pp. 27, 91, 193.

In: U.S. Family Planning … ISBN: 978-1-62618-532-6
Editors: E.A. Rivera and D.R. Murphy

Chapter 3

THE U.N. POPULATION FUND: BACKGROUND AND THE U.S. FUNDING DEBATE*

Luisa Blanchfield

SUMMARY

The United Nations Population Fund (UNFPA), established in 1969, is the world's largest source of population and reproductive health programs and the principal unit within the United Nations for global population issues. In 2009, the organization provided services in 155 developing and transition countries, with funds totaling $783.1 million, drawn primarily from voluntary contributions made by nations and some foundations.

The United States, with strong support from Congress, was an important actor in the launch of UNFPA in 1969. During the mid-to-late 1960s, Congress began to express heightened concern over the impact of rapid population growth on development prospects in poor countries. In 1967, Congress earmarked funds for population assistance programs, urging the United States to channel family planning resources through the United Nations and other international organizations.

* This is an edited, reformatted and augmented version of a Congressional Research Service publication, RL32703, dated July 15, 2010.

Since it was established, UNFPA has transitioned from an organization focused on statistical collection and analysis to an agency providing maternal and child health/family planning assistance. UNFPA played a large role in shaping the 1994 International Conference on Population and Development, held in Cairo. The Cairo Conference marked a turning point in the international debate over the impact of population issues on global development, and established a policy framework called the Plan of Action that continues to guide current family planning and reproductive health policies, including the work of UNFPA. The Plan integrated population concerns into the broad context of development—concluding that education and health, including reproductive health, were prerequisites for sustainable development.

In the past three decades, there has been continuing and contentious debate within the United States, especially among Members of Congress, as to whether the United States should financially support UNFPA. This debate has centered on the extent to which, if any, UNFPA aids China's coercive family planning programs and policies. In 15 of the past 25 years, the United States did not contribute to the organization as a result of executive branch determinations that UNFPA's program in China violated the "Kemp-Kasten" amendment, which bans U.S. aid to organizations involved in the management of coercive family planning programs. From FY2002 through FY2008, the George W. Bush Administration found UNFPA ineligible for funding under the Kemp-Kasten amendment.

In March 2009, President Barack Obama expressed his support for UNFPA and announced that the United States would contribute $50 million to the organization as directed in the Omnibus Appropriations Act, 2009 (P.L. 111-8). On December 16, 2009, President Obama signed the Consolidated Appropriations Act, 2010 (P.L. 111-117). Division F of that bill, the Department of State, Foreign Operations, and Related Programs Appropriations Act, 2010, directed that $55 million should be made available for UNFPA. For FY2011, the Obama Administration requested $50 million for U.S. contributions to UNFPA, which would be drawn from the International Organizations and Programs account (IO&P).

While UNFPA receives voluntary contributions from many countries and some private foundations, most of its income comes from a handful of donors. The Netherlands, Sweden, and Japan have consistently been the largest contributors. In 2009, the U.S. contribution to UNFPA was the fourth-largest donation, representing approximately 9.5% of UNFPA's annual regular budget.

Introduction

The United Nations Population Fund (UNFPA), which began operations in 1969 as the U.N. Fund for Population Activities, is the world's largest source of population and reproductive health programs and the principal unit within the United Nations for global population issues. In 2009, the organization provided services in 155 developing and transition countries, with funds totaling $783.1 million, drawn exclusively from voluntary contributions made by governments and some foundations. In the past three decades, there has been continuing and contentious debate within the United States, and especially among Members of Congress, as to whether the United States should financially contribute to UNFPA. The debate has centered on the extent to which, if any, UNFPA aids China's coercive family planning programs and policies. In 15 of the past 25 years, the United States has been one of the leading contributors to UNFPA. For the other years, the United States withheld funding to the organization through the so-called "Kemp-Kasten" amendment that has been included in foreign operations appropriations since FY1985. Kemp-Kasten states that U.S. funds will not be made available to any organization or program which, as determined by the President, supports or participates in the management of a program of coercive abortion or involuntary sterilization. U.S. contributions to UNFPA will likely be considered during the second session of the 111th Congress as part of the debate on the annual State-Foreign Operations appropriations bill and other related legislation. From FY2002 through FY2008, the George W. Bush Administration found UNFPA ineligible for U.S. funding under Kemp-Kasten and transferred proposed annual contributions to other foreign aid activities. In March 2009, President Barack Obama announced that the United States would resume U.S. contributions to UNFPA, specifying that $50 million would be made available to the organization as directed in the Omnibus Appropriations Act, 2009 (P.L. 111-8). In FY2010, the United States provided $55 million to UNFPA as required by Division F of the Consolidated Appropriations Act, 2010 (P.L. 111-117). For FY2011, the President requested that the United States contribute $50 million to the organization. This chapter provides an overview of the U.N. Population Fund, its current mission and operations, and recent funding trends. It further discusses the role of the United States in supporting UNFPA programs, the varying interpretations by several Administrations of legislative authorities pertaining to UNFPA's eligibility for U.S. resources, and congressional debates over how much and under what conditions the United States should voluntarily contribute to UNFPA. Finally, it reviews the findings of several private and U.S. government investigations of China's family planning programs and the role UNFPA plays in their implementation.

UNFPA: Origins and Operations

The United Nations, since its earliest days, has maintained an interest in population issues. In 1947, the United Nations established a Population Commission that collected and analyzed global population data and supported member government efforts to examine information about national populations. Following several years of U.N. debate over the rapid rise of the world's population, the General Assembly approved a resolution in 1966 calling on the United Nations and other international organizations to extend technical assistance on population matters. In 1967, the U.N. Secretary-General created a Trust Fund for Population Activities, which in 1969 was renamed the U.N. Fund for Population Activities (UNFPA). Initially, UNFPA was administered by the United Nations Development Program (UNDP), the organization's primary international development organ. Within a few years, at the direction of the General Assembly, UNFPA had expanded its operations beyond statistical collection and analysis to the provision of maternal and child health/family planning, communication and education, and population policy assistance. By 1972, UNFPA was operating in 78 countries with a budget of over $30 million. With such rapid growth in the Fund's scope and programs, UNFPA became a separate entity under the direct authority of the General Assembly, with the same status as UNDP and the U.N. Children's Fund (UNICEF).[1] In these initial years, the United States provided the majority of UNFPA funding through voluntary contributions. In 1968 and 1969, when seven governments extended financial support, the $4 million transfer by the United States represented nearly 80% of total contributions. By 1972, the number of donors had grown to 52, but the United States remained by far the largest source of funds, with 46% of the total. Over the next decade, the U.S. share declined to about 25% as other nations increased their contributions.

UNFPA and World Population Conferences: 1974 and 1984

UNFPA played a significant role in the World Population Conferences, held a decade apart in Bucharest (1974) and Mexico City (1984). Following the 1974 meeting of 133 nations, the U.N. General Assembly called for the expansion of international population assistance, with UNFPA taking a lead role, to implement the plan of action endorsed at the Bucharest Conference. Partially due to the growing attention on world population issues, UNFPA operations expanded rapidly during this period. The scope of UNFPA's work also broadened, so that by the early 1980s, the organization focused on eight primary areas:

- family planning, including delivery systems and fertility regulation techniques;
- data collection;
- formulation and evaluation of population policies and programs;
- communications and education;
- population dynamics, including demographic projections and their analysis;
- implementation of policies and programs, including efforts "beyond family planning" related to law and population, status of women, and economic policies;
- special programs focusing on women, children, the elderly, the disabled, and programs to promote social justice; and
- multisector activities, including support for population conferences and training.[2]

The 1994 Cairo Conference and UNFPA's Changing Mandate

UNFPA was a major catalyst in organizing, financing, and implementing outcomes of the 1994 International Conference on Population and Development (ICPD), held in Cairo. The Cairo Conference marked a turning point in the international debate over the impact of population issues on global development and established a policy framework that continues to guide current family planning and reproductive health policies. The Plan of Action that emerged from the Cairo Conference, to a much greater extent than before, integrated population concerns into the broad context of development, concluding that education and health (including reproductive health), were prerequisites for sustainable development. The Conference shifted population program strategies away from demographic goals and toward human welfare and poverty reduction objectives. The Conference further focused far more attention on the status and empowerment of women. Moving beyond strictly health issues, the conference endorsed programs to promote expanded opportunities for the education of women and girls, to end gender discrimination and violence against women, and to strengthen women's grassroots activist organizations.[3]

Since the Cairo Conference, UNFPA programs have and continue to be guided by the ICPD's Program of Action, which contains several goals, including universal access to reproductive health services by 2015; universal primary education and closing the gender gap in education by 2015; reducing maternal mortality by 75% by 2015; reducing infant mortality; and increasing life expectancy. In 1999, an additional goal—reducing HIV infection rates in persons 15-24 years of age by 25% in the most-affected countries by 2005 and by 25% globally by 2010—was incorporated into the Program of Action and integrated into UNFPA's work.[4]

UNFPA Operations Today

UNFPA is headquartered in New York City and supports five regional, six sub-regional, and 129 field offices worldwide. It has approximately 1,119 staff members and in 2009 operated in 155 countries, areas, and territories.[5]

In 2009, UNFPA's total income was $783.1 million, a decrease of approximately $62 million from 2008 (see **Table 1**). The organization attributes this decline to the global economic downturn. UNFPA derives most of its income from voluntary contributions to its regular budget which finances continuing core country programs and the organization's administrative costs. A growing but less flexible source of revenue has been from supplementary donations that are provided either for cost-sharing purposes or for placement in trust funds. Through supplementary resource transfers, donors can earmark exactly how their contributions will be spent. In 2000, for example, the Netherlands provided $41 million specifically to procure contraceptive commodities.

While UNFPA receives voluntary contributions from many countries and from some private foundations, most of its income for regular country programs and operating expenses comes from a handful of donors. In the past eight years, approximately 60% to 75% of UNFPA's regular income has come from six country donors (see **Table 2**). The Netherlands and Japan have consistently been the largest contributors. In 2009, the first year the United States contributed to UNFPA since 2001, it was the fourth-largest donor, representing approximately 9.5% of the UNFPA regular budget.

UNFPA Program Priorities

Currently, UNFPA activities focus on seven program areas that support the broad strategy of improving reproductive health:

- **Preventing HIV/AIDS**—promoting safer sexual behavior among young people, ensuring that condoms are available and widely and correctly used, empowering women to protect themselves and their children, and encouraging men to take responsibility for preventing the spread of HIV/AIDS;
- **Making motherhood safer**—expanding the availability of emergency obstetric care for women who develop complications, having skilled workers available, and meeting unmet needs for contraceptive services;
- **Supporting young people**—providing accurate information, counseling, and services to prevent unwanted pregnancies and sexually transmitted diseases;
- **Promoting gender equality**—promoting legal and policy reforms, supporting gender-sensitive data collection, and backing programs that empower women economically;
- **Assisting in emergencies**—providing supplies and services to protect reproductive health during disasters;
- **Securing reproductive health supplies**—coordinating the delivery of supplies, forecasting needs, and building logistical capacity at the country level; and
- **Preventing and treating obstetric fistula**[6]—providing access to medical care, increasing education and family planning services, postponing pregnancy for young girls, improving girls' nutrition, and repairing physical and emotional damage.[7]

In the years since the Cairo Conference, UNFPA has allocated roughly 60% of its annual resources to reproductive health and family planning service programs and 20% to strategies for population and development.

The balance of UNFPA spending focuses on coordinating activities, gender equity, and women's empowerment programs.[8] (See **Figure 1** for UNFPA program functions in 2009.)

Table 1. UNFPA Income, 1997 to 2009 (current $ in millions)

Year	Regular	Supplemental	Total
1997	$293	$33	$326
1998	$273	$36	$309
1999	$250	$38	$288
2000	$262	$104	$366
2001	$268	$128	$396
2002	$260	$113	$373
2003	$292	$106	$398
2004	$332	$174	$506
2005	$366	$199	$565
2006	$389	$216	$605
2007	$457	$295	$752
2008	$469	$376	$845
2009	$486	$297	$783

Source: UNFPA annual reports.

Table 2. UNFPA Major Contributors, 2000 to 2009 (contribution as a % of UNFPA regular income)

	2000	2001	2002	2003	2004	2005	2006	2007	2008	2009
Netherlands	19.3 %	18.8 %	21.1 %	23.1 %	21.8 %	20.8 %	19.3 %	17.5 %	16.1 %	16.6 %
Japan	18.4 %	18.2 %	15.2 %	13.5 %	11.9 %	10.2 %	8.5 %	7.3 %	6.3 %	6.2 %
Norway	8.8 %	9.0 %	9.7 %	11.3 %	10.0 %	10.3 %	10.5 %	12.8 %	10.1 %	9.9 %
Denmark	9.1 %	8.8 %	8.7 %	8.7 %	8.9 %	8.4%	8.0 %	7.1%	10.2 %	8.1 %
U.K.	8.5 %	8.2 %	10.2 %	10.3 %	11.1 %	10.0 %	9.7 %	8.8 %	6.5 %	7.1 %
Sweden	7.1 %	6.2 %	7.3 %	8.2 %	10.8 %	13.3 %	14.2 %	13.3 %	13 %	12.1 %
United States	8.2 %	8.0 %	0.0 %	0.0 %	0.0 %	0.0 %	0.0 %	0.0 %	0.0 %	9.5 %

Regional and Country Program Focus

Over the past decade, roughly 33% of UNFPA programs have been carried out in sub-Saharan Africa, with an additional 28% focused in Asia. In 2009, UNFPA maintained its largest program in Sudan ($19.90 million), followed by Ethiopia ($16.38 million), and the Democratic Republic of the Congo ($16.32 million). (See **Figure 2** for UNFPA assistance by region in 2009.) UNFPA program expenditures in China have ranged between $4 million and $6 million annually in recent years. In 2009, UNFPA contributed approximately $4.57 million to projects in China. In 2008, it contributed $6.76 million.

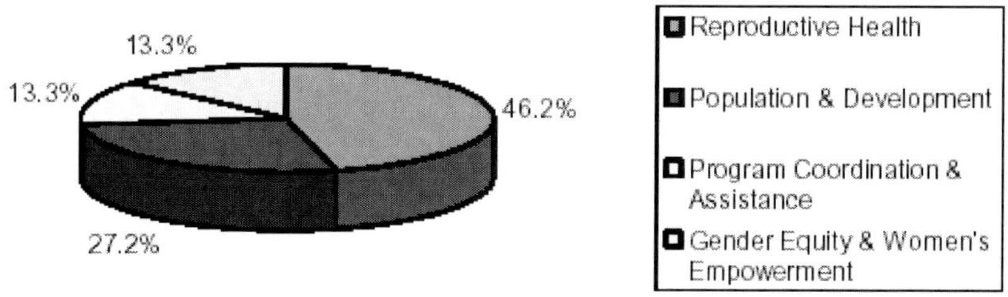

Source: UNFPA Annual Report, 2009.

Figure 1. UNFPA Program Functions, 2009.

U.S. Policy Towards UNFPA

The United States was an important actor in the launch of UNFPA in 1969. During the mid-to-late 1960s, Congress began to express heightened concern over the impact of rapid population growth on development prospects in poor countries, noting that the world's population was growing by about 2% annually compared with only a 1% growth in food production. In 1967, for the first time, Congress amended the Foreign Assistance Act of 1961 to specifically authorize and earmark funds for population assistance programs, urging the United States especially to channel family planning resources through the United Nations and other international organizations. Some Members believed that such earmarks were necessary because the State Department and the U.S. Agency for International Development (USAID) had not been giving the issue adequate attention.[9]

These initial U.S. contributions, however, were conditioned on the requirement that other donors match the American payment in an equal amount. This incentive helped UNFPA exceed its 1970 projected resource goal when 22 other countries contributed a combined $7.7 million. In 1971, with the same matching requirement tied to the U.S. pledge of $15 million, UNFPA received donations of $14.5 million from 45 nations.[10] As shown in

Table 3, U.S. contributions continued to climb throughout the 1970s and early 1980s. At the same time, however, the number and size of transfers from other donors rose faster, so that the share of UNFPA resources from the United States declined from 50% to around 27%.

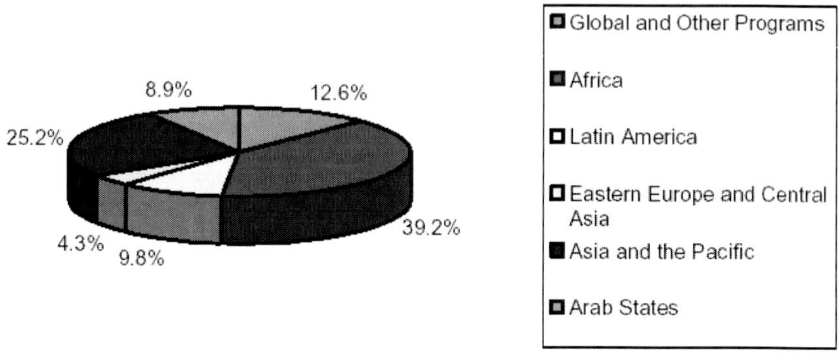

Source: UNFPA Annual Report, 2009.

Figure 2. UNFPA Assistance by Region, 2009.

In FY2009, the U.S. contribution to UNFPA peaked at $50 million. For FY2010, UNFPA is expected to receive $55 million from the United States, the largest U.S. contribution to date. The highest UNFPA contribution earmarked by Congress prior to FY2009—$46 million—was enacted in the FY1985 foreign aid appropriation, P.L. 98-461. However, only a portion of these funds—$36 million—was transferred to the organization as U.S. policy and its support for UNFPA shifted.

1984 Review of U.S. Funding for UNFPA

In August 1984, government representatives from around the world met in Mexico City for the 2nd U.N. International Conference on Population. At the conference, the Ronald Reagan Administration announced new eligibility requirements for organizations receiving U.S. bilateral population assistance funds. The new policy stipulated that no non-governmental organizations (NGOs) that received population assistance funding from the United States could actively promote or perform abortion as a family planning method in other countries. This change became known as the "Mexico City policy" and was applied by the Reagan and George H.W. Bush Administrations for nine years, reversed by President Bill Clinton in 1993, and reinstituted by President George W. Bush in 2001.[11]

Table 3. U.S. Contributions to UNFPA, FY1968-FY2010 (current $ in millions)

Fiscal Year	U.S. Contribution	% of Total UNFPA Funds	Fiscal Year	U.S. Contribution	% of Total UNFPA Funds
1968	$1.7	79.3%	**1990**	$0.0	—
1969	$2.3	79.3%	**1991**	$0.0	—
1970	$7.5	50.0%	**1992**	$0.0	—
1971	$14.2	50.0%	**1993**	$0.0	—
1972	$14.0	46.1%	**1994**	$40.0	15.1%
1973	$17.9	42.2%	**1995**	$35.0	11.2%
1974	$20.0	37.0%	**1996**	$22.8	7.4%
1975	$20.0	31.7%	**1997**	$25.0	8.6%
1976	$20.0	25.2%	**1998**	$20.0	7.2%
1977	$29.0	31.6%	**1999**	$0.0	—
1978	$28.0	27.2%	**2000**	$21.5	8.1%
1979	$30.0	26.7%	**2001**	$21.5	8.0%
1980	$32.0	25.7%	**2002**	$0.0	—
1981	$32.0	26.3%	**2003**	$0.0	—
1982	$33.8	26.1%	**2004**	$0.0	—
1983	$33.8	26.1%	**2005**	$0.0	—
1984	$38.2	27.5%	**2006**	$0.0	—
1985	$36.0	27.3%	**2007**	$0.0	—
1986	$0.0	—	**2008**	$0.0	—
1987	$0.0	—	**2009**	$50.0	9.5%
1988	$0.0	—	**2010**	$55.0	To be determined

Sources: Department of State, USAID, and CRS percentage calculations.

Also at the 1984 Mexico City Conference, the Reagan Administration announced it would establish requirements for UNFPA to provide assurances that the organization was not engaged in, or was not providing funds for, abortion or coercive family planning programs. Concerns focused on

UNFPA's activities related to China's coercive family planning practices. UNFPA had launched its first program in China in 1980, focusing largely on increasing Beijing's capacity for data collection and improving maternal and child health and family planning services. At the time, the Administration reportedly held up $19 million (of $38 million allocated for UNFPA for FY1984) until the organization could provide the necessary assurances. These funds were released later in FY1984.

Following the Mexico City Conference, attention returned to the FY1985 UNFPA earmark of $46 million and how much the United States should transfer, given the new White House policy. USAID, which at the time maintained responsibility for managing UNFPA contributions, undertook a review in early 1985 of UNFPA's program, especially in China, to determine whether the organization was involved in any way with involuntary abortions.[12] In March 1985 that review found that UNFPA did not include involuntary abortion as part of its programs, and therefore did not violate legislative restrictions or conditions announced at the Mexico City Conference on funding organizations engaged in involuntary practices.[13]

As a result, UNFPA remained eligible for U.S. support but did not receive the full earmarked amount of $46 million. On March 30, 1985, USAID contributed $36 million to UNFPA, withholding $10 million "to express United States disapproval of coercion in the implementation of the China population control program."[14] The $10 million matched roughly the amount UNFPA spent annually in China. Because AID wanted to re-program the $10 million for other bilateral population assistance programs, the Administration needed to overcome the specific legislative earmark of $46 million in the FY1985 appropriation. Accordingly, the White House requested authority as part of an FY1985 supplemental appropriation submission to shift $10 million from UNFPA to other population aid groups.

The Kemp-Kasten Amendment

Rather than approve the Reagan Administration's request for authority to transfer the $10 million from UNFPA, Congress agreed to the "Kemp-Kasten" amendment as part of the FY1985 Supplemental Appropriations bill, H.R. 2577.[15] The amendment states that U.S. funds would not be made available to "any organization or program which, as determined by the President, supports or participates in the management of a program of coercive abortion or involuntary sterilization."[16] The House Appropriations Committee did not provide details on what was meant by the phrase, "support or participate in the management" of a program. However, in the "additional views" section of the Committee Report, Representativc Jack Kemp stated that management of coercive programs may include providing resources to collect and analyze data necessary to the enforcement of such a program; training of the individuals who plan, manage, and carry out such a program, education and publicity about the programs; assistance to the official bodies of government that are charged with developing and implementing such a program; and other such assistance.[17]

Congressman Kemp also stated that the amendment would most likely affect U.S. funding of the UNFPA, "because of its involvement with the program of coercive abortion in the People's Republic of China."[18] The Kemp-Kasten amendment was enacted on August 15, 1985, as part of the FY1985 Supplemental Appropriations Act (P.L. 99-88).

Implementation and Court Challenges

Despite the directive from the amendment that the President, or alternatively the Secretary of State, issue any determination regarding the Kemp-Kasten amendment, President Reagan delegated his authority to the Secretary of State on September 19, 1985,[19] who in turn authorized the re-delegation of this authority to the Director of the International Development Cooperation Agency (IDCA).[20] On September 25, 1985, IDCA Administrator Peter McPherson announced the Administration's determination that UNFPA, because of its activities in China, was participating in the management of a program of coercive abortion and involuntary sterilization. In letters to congressional leaders, Administrator McPherson cited Representative Kemp's interpretation, as set out in his additional views in H.Rept. 99-142, of what characterized the participation of an organization in a coercive abortion program. The Administrator concluded that China's "one-child- per-couple policy has resulted in coerced abortion and involuntary sterilization."[21]

The Reagan Administrator further announced that since the Kemp-Kasten amendment and his determination under it now superseded the $46 million UNFPA earmark for FY1985, USAID would reprogram $10 million for voluntary family planning programs for use elsewhere in the world. He also stated that if Kemp-Inouye was enacted again in FY1986, UNFPA could receive funds under only three conditions: (1) UNFPA withdraws its program from China; (2) China would begin to punish abuses concerning coercive abortion and involuntary sterilizations; or (3) UNFPA "radically" changes its program in China, such as by supplying only contraceptive materials.[22]

Almost immediately, the Population Institute, an NGO, filed suit against Administrator McPherson and the U.S. government to block the redirection of UNFPA funds and invalidate the determination. On August 12, 1986, the Court upheld the Administration's decision to withhold UNFPA funding.

From 1986 to 1992, USAID continued to request funds for UNFPA, although with the understanding that a decision on whether to transfer the money would be reviewed under the terms of the Kemp-Kasten amendment, which Congress also continued to enact each year in the foreign assistance appropriations. In each year, USAID found that UNFPA was ineligible for U.S. support.

Reinterpretation of Kemp-Kasten by the Clinton Administration

The issue of coercive practices within China's family planning program and the role of UNFPA remained controversial throughout the Clinton Administration. As one of his first acts as chief executive, President Clinton reversed the Mexico City policy of Presidents Reagan and Bush, and issued a determination finding that UNFPA programs in China did not violate the terms of Kemp-Kasten. The policy reversal was based on several factors, including the following:

- **Ambiguity of the Kemp-Kasten language**—The Administration noted that the Court of Appeals, in considering the case brought by the Population Institute, deferred to the USAID interpretation of Kemp-Kasten because it was a "reasonable reading of an ambiguous provision and did not otherwise conflict with the expressed intention of Congress." The Administration argued that because of this ambiguity, the new Administration had a right to interpret Kemp-Kasten for itself.
- **Over-reliance on the 1985 statements by Representative Kemp**—The Admin-istration pointed especially to the 1985 Court of Appeals opinion that questioned the relevance of the additional views of Representative Kemp interpreting the Kemp-Inouye amendment. The Court observed that, although the Administration considered Representative Kemp's remarks as the clearest explanation of an "ambiguous term," Congressman Kemp could not convince his colleagues to adopt his views in the committee report itself.

- **Focus should be on the terms "coercive" and "involuntary" and the intent of the organization in question**—The Clinton Administration believed that it was reasonable to apply the Kemp-Kasten restrictions only in cases where the organization knowingly and intentionally provided direct support for, or helped manage people or agencies who were clearly engaged in, coercive abortion or involuntary sterilization. The Administration concluded that although it remained concerned about coercive practices in China, it believed that UNFPA did not "knowingly" or "intentionally" support directly such practices.[23]

Congress continued to include Kemp-Kasten language in Foreign Operations Appropriations acts, and in most years attached additional conditions on UNFPA contributions that required the organization to (1) keep U.S. funds in a separate account, (2) not spend U.S. money in China, and (3) to forego transfers from the United States equal to the amount UNFPA allocated for its China program. In some years, the United States withheld about $3.5 million from UNFPA, an amount that approximated the size of UNFPA's expenditures in China.

For a brief period in 1997, the controversy over whether to fund UNFPA subsided when UNFPA's program in China expired and new activities did not resume immediately. Nevertheless, despite opposition from the United States, UNFPA re-established a program in China, and in FY1999 appropriation legislation, Congress prohibited all U.S. contributions to the organization. Congress restored funding in FY2000, but with the requirement that an amount equal to UNFPA expenditures in China be withheld. This resulted in a $3.5 million deduction in FY2000 and FY2001. (See the **Appendix** for details on Administration actions and legislative restrictions regarding UNFPA funding from FY1985 to FY2011.)

George W. Bush Administration and the Kemp-Kasten Amendment

The first budget submitted by President Bush for FY2002 included a proposed $25 million U.S. contribution to UNFPA. While the new Administration reinstated the so-called "Mexico City policy" restrictions that applied to bilateral family planning funds, there was no indication of a change in policy regarding UNFPA and the Kemp-Kasten conditions attached to U.S.

contributions. Subsequently, in the FY2002 Foreign Operations Appropriations, Congress provided "not more than" $34 million for UNFPA. Although such language represented a ceiling for the amount of funds for UNFPA, as opposed to a floor, or minimum amount that must be provided, the language was similar to prior year Foreign Operations bills that had been fulfilled by the Clinton Administration, minus the withholding requirement.

However, in the face of the conflicting evidence released in late 2001 by the Guy and Biegman investigation teams (see section "UNFPA and China" for further details on the group's findings), in mid-January 2002, the White House placed a hold on U.S. contributions to UNFPA pending a review of the organization's program in China.

In a statement before the Senate Foreign Relations Committee on February 27, 2002, Assistant Secretary of State for Population, Refugees and Migration Arthur Dewey noted that the legislative text regarding UNFPA funding—"not more than $34 million"—gave the Administration considerable discretion over exactly how much to provide UNFPA. While stating that the United States supported UNFPA's work worldwide to provide safe and voluntary family planning, enhance maternal and infant health, and prevent the spread of HIV/AIDS, the Administration remained concerned about periodic reports of abuse and coercion in China's family planning program. Given new information and the requirements of the Kemp-Kasten amendment, Assistant Secretary Dewey argued that the State Department was obligated to investigate the matter further before releasing any funds in FY2002.[24]

State Department Assessment and Findings

The State Department sent an investigation team to China for a two-week review of UNFPA programs on May 13, 2002. The team was led by former Ambassador William Brown, and included Bonnie Glick, a former State Department official, and Dr. Theodore Tong, a public health professor at the University of Arizona. The State Department's assessment team filed its report with Secretary Powell on May 29, making a series of findings and recommendations.[25] The group found that

- there was no evidence that UNFPA "has knowingly supported or participated in the management of a program of coercive abortion or involuntary sterilization" in China;
- despite some relaxation of government restrictions in counties where UNFPA operates, China maintained coercive elements in its population programs in law and practice; and

- Chinese leaders viewed "population control as a high priority" and remained concerned over implications for socioeconomic change.

On the basis of these findings, Ambassador Brown and his colleagues recommended that (1) the United States should release not more than $34 million of previously appropriated funds to UNFPA; (2) until China ends all forms of coercion in law and practice, no U.S. government funds should be allocated to population programs in China; and (3) appropriate resources, possibly from the United States, should be allocated to monitor and evaluate Chinese population control programs.

UNFPA Found in Violation of Kemp-Kasten by the Bush Administration

President Bush withheld U.S. funding from UNFPA from FY2002 through FY2008 due to concerns that the organization supported or participated in what the Administration viewed as a program of coercive abortion and involuntary sterilization in China.

These decisions were made in response to the findings and recommendations of the Brown investigation. The Administration consistently maintained that it would be willing to reconsider its position if UNFPA ended its program in China or if the program was restructured in a way consistent with U.S. law.[26]

On July 22, 2002, then-Secretary of State Powell, to whom President Bush had delegated the decision, announced that UNFPA remained in violation of Kemp-Kasten and ineligible for U.S. funding. The State Department's analysis of the Secretary's determination found that even though UNFPA did not "knowingly" support or participate in a coercive practice, that alone would not preclude the application of Kemp-Kasten.

Instead, a finding that the recipient of U.S. funds—in this case UNFPA—simply supports or participates in such a program, whether knowingly or unknowingly, would trigger the restriction. The assessment team found that the Chinese government imposes fines and penalties on families ("social compensation fees") that have children exceeding the number approved by the government.

The Department further noted that UNFPA had funded computers and data-processing equipment that had helped strengthen the management of the Chinese State Family Planning Commission. Beyond the legitimate uses of these and other items financed by UNFPA, such equipment facilitated, in the view of the State Department, China's ability to impose social compensation fees or perform abortions by coercion.

The State Department analysis concluded that UNFPA's involvement in China's family planning program "allows the Chinese government to implement more effectively its program of coercive abortion."[27]

Obama Administration Kemp-Kasten Determination

President Barack Obama has expressed his support for UNFPA. On March 24, 2009, a State Department spokesperson confirmed that the U.S. government would contribute $50 million to UNFPA in FY2009 as provided by the Omnibus Appropriations Act, 2009 (P.L. 111-8). This decision, according to Administration officials, highlights the President's "strong commitment" to international family planning, women's health, and global development.[28] In FY2010 and FY2011, the President requested that the United States contribute $50 million to UNFPA during each fiscal year.

Legislative Action, FY2009 through FY2011

This section addresses the most recent legislative actions regarding U.S. contributions to UNFPA. See the **Appendix** for a description of Administration activities and legislative actions since 1985.

FY2011 Request

For FY2011, the Obama Administration requested $50 million for U.S. contributions to UNFPA, which would be drawn from the International Organizations and Programs account (IO&P). This contribution, according to the Administration, would place the United States in line with other top UNFPA donors and "signal strong support" for the organization When putting forth its request, the Administration also emphasized that UNFPA does not support abortion as a means of family planning.[29]

FY2010 Administration Request and Appropriations

On December 16, 2009, President Obama signed the Consolidated Appropriations Act, 2010 (P.L. 111-117). Division F of that bill, the Department of State, Foreign Operations, and Related Programs Appropriations Act, 2010, directed that $55 million shall be made available for UNFPA under the International Organizations and Programs (IO&P) account. As in previous years, certain conditions applied, including that

- none of the funds made available may be used by UNFPA for a country program in China;
- U.S. contributions to UNFPA must be kept in an account separate from other accounts at UNFPA and should not commingle with other sums; and
- for UNFPA to receive U.S. funding, it must not fund abortions.

The bill also established related reporting requirements for the Secretary of State. Not later than four months after the enactment of the act, the Secretary was required to submit a report to the Committees on Appropriations indicating the funds UNFPA is budgeting for a country program in China. If the Secretary's report indicated that funds will be spent on such a program, then the amount of such funds shall be deducted from the funds made available to UNFPA for the remainder of the fiscal year in which the report is submitted.

For FY2010, the Obama Administration had requested that the United States contribute $50 million to UNFPA under the IO&P account. [30]

FY2009 Appropriations

On March 11, 2009, President Obama signed the Omnibus Appropriations Act, 2009 (P.L. 111-8). Division H of that bill, the Department of State, Foreign Operations, and Related Programs Appropriations Act, 2009, allocated $50 million for UNFPA.

It specified that not more than $30 million of this amount should be derived from the IO&P account. The remaining amount should be made available from the Global Health and Child Survival (GHCS) account.

In addition, Section 7079 of P.L. 111-8 established a number of conditions for U.S. contributions to UNFPA. Specifically, none of the funds made available should be used by UNFPA for a country program in China.[31] In addition:

- Funds appropriated by the act "that are not made available because of the operation of any provision of law, shall be made available to UNFPA notwithstanding any such provision of law." Some expressed concern that this provision takes away the authority of the President to determine whether UNFPA is eligible for U.S. contributions under the Kemp-Kasten amendment.
- U.S. contributions to UNFPA shall be made available for specific purposes, including (1) providing and distributing safe equipment,

medicine and supplies; (2) supplying contraceptives to prevent unintended pregnancies and the spread of sexually transmitted diseases; (3) preventing and treating obstetric fistula; (4) reestablishing maternal health services in areas with poor infrastructure; (5) promoting the abandonment of female genital cutting; and (6) promoting access to basic services such as water, sanitation, food, and health care.

- U.S. contributions to UNFPA must be kept in a separate account by the organization and should not commingle with other sums.
- For UNFPA to receive U.S. funding, it must not fund abortions.

On March 24, 2009, the Obama Administration announced that the United States would contribute $50 million (as directed in P.L. 111-8) to UNFPA under the Kemp-Kasten amendment.

The Bush Administration had previously requested $25 million for UNFPA funding if the organization was deemed eligible under the Kemp-Kasten amendment. The funds would be appropriated under the Child Survival and Health Programs account.[32]

UNFPA and China

One issue that has been debated among many Members of Congress and past and current Administrations involves whether, and to what extent, UNFPA programs in China violate the Kemp-Kasten amendment. As previously mentioned, initial UNFPA programs in China concentrated on bolstering China's capacity for data collection and analysis, and maternal and child health/family planning activities. Following the Cairo population conference in 1994 and the conclusion of UNFPA's third Chinese program, UNFPA and Beijing officials began to discuss significant changes for a fourth agreement that would more closely follow the principles set out in Cairo.

The subsequent UNFPA program, launched in 1998, concentrated efforts in 32 counties where birth targets and quotas had been eliminated by the Chinese government.

The fourth program shifted from a more administrative family planning approach—focusing on population control and imposed contraceptive methods and orders—to an "integrated, client-oriented reproductive health approach in the project counties" that included education and counseling regarding informed choice of contraceptive methods and reproductive health rights.

According to UNFPA, service delivery points were upgraded to offer integrated reproductive health services in both the Chinese State Family Planning Commission and the Ministry of Health.

UNFPA said that there had been a "downward trend" in the abortion ratio in these counties, and that the organization had played a "catalytic role in introducing a comprehensive, voluntary reproductive health approach," that included rigorous monitoring of the projects.[33] The fifth program, covering the period 2003-2005, expanded many of the earlier initiatives.

In June 2005, UNFPA approved a sixth program for China that began in 2006 and spans five years. The $27 million program is to build on the policy changes made in 1998 and includes two components. The reproductive health element seeks to increase the utilization of high-quality, client-centered, gender-sensitive reproductive health and family planning services, and to reduce the vulnerability and risk behavior associated with HIV/AIDS among migrants, young people, and other vulnerable groups.

The population and development component centers on strengthening the government's capacity for addressing population-related policies, especially those regarding gender, migration, and aging issues, and enhancing the government's ability to collect and apply surveillance data, particularly data related to HIV/AIDS.[34]

Investigations of UNFPA Programs in China

During implementation of the fourth and fifth programs, UNFPA's operations in China have been closely scrutinized by several investigatory teams, including one dispatched by the State Department in 2002.

Most of these groups concluded that UNFPA was not involved in supporting coercive or involuntary family planning programs in China, although one—sponsored by the Population Research Institute (PRI)—concluded otherwise.

These conflicting reports, together with continuing reviews of UNFPA practices in China and varying interpretations by U.S. officials, sparked renewed controversy and extensive congressional debate beginning in 2001 over the appropriate role of the United States in financially supporting UNFPA operations worldwide. The four non-U.S. government sponsored investigations came to the following conclusions.

The Population Research Institute

PRI's report concluded that UNFPA "directly supports coercive family planning with funding, and through its complicity with the implementation of policies which are fundamentally coercive in principle and practice." The PRI team, led by Josephine Guy, spent four days in Sihui County, Guangdong Province, in late September 2001, conducting numerous interviews with alleged victims and witnesses of coercive practices.

According to the team's interview notes and videos, non-voluntary abortions and use of IUDs, mandatory examinations, and punishment for noncompliance—both imprisonment and economic fines—continued in this county which was among the 32 in which UNFPA supported programs.[35]

The Biegman Group

This team found that UNFPA plays a "positive and important catalytic role in the reform of reproductive health and family planning services in China" and in moving China away from coercive family planning practices and abuses. It recommended that UNFPA continue its program in China and expand its scope and resources in the future.[36]

This UNFPA-sponsored review team, led by Ambassador Nicolaas Biegman, former Dutch Ambassador to the U.N. and including diplomats from Honduras, the Czech Republic, and Botswana, conducted a six-day investigation in October 2001, interviewing officials and visiting sites in Beijing and in Sihui and Qianjiang Counties.

British All-Party Parliamentary Group on Population, Development, and Reproductive Health

The British parliamentary team found that although problems remain in some parts of China regarding reproductive rights, the Chinese government was "moving in the right direction, with the support of UNFPA."

The bi-partisan group spent a week in Beijing and Yunnan Province in April 2002, reporting that UNFPA programs were having a "positive effect" in reforming Chinese reproductive health services and offering women "a choice over their own lives."[37]

The Interfaith Delegation to China

This group returned from a September 2003 visit finding, among other things, that the Chinese government was taking steps to end coercive family planning practices, that UNFPA was a major force in China's transition to voluntary policies, and that UNFPA did not support or participate in managing China's family planning program.

While the group acknowledged that in such a brief trip it could not gain a comprehensive view of China's family planning activities or the work of UNFPA, it felt confident in recommending that the United States should maintain a policy of constructive engagement with China regarding family planning matters, and that U.S. funding for UNFPA should be restored, and the Kemp-Kasten amendment revised.

The nine-member mission was sponsored by Catholics for a Free Choice.[38]

POSSIBLE KEMP-KASTEN APPLICATION BEYOND UNFPA

Critics of the Administration policy, including some Members of Congress, have expressed concern over what they perceive to be a shift in the interpretation of Kemp-Kasten restrictions related to UNFPA and other international organizations.

They point to a USAID notification to the Global Health Council that the agency would not provide funding for the Council's 31st annual meeting in June 2004 because UNFPA would be a participant. Some believe that this represented a State Department warning to UNICEF, the World Health Organization, and other organizations that continued involvement in joint programs with UNFPA might jeopardize their funding support from the United States.[39]

In 2003, the State Department decided that it would fund a $1 million HIV/AIDS program supporting African and Asian refugees only if the implementing NGO group—Reproductive Health for Refugees Consortium—did not include Marie Stopes International among its members. Marie Stopes International is a British-based reproductive health organization that is also a major implementing partner of UNFPA in China.

The State Department, while not making a legal determination under the Kemp-Kasten amendment, felt that an action not to fund Marie Stopes International would be the "approach most consistent with U.S. policy."[40] On August 11, 2003, however, the Consortium declined to accept the $1 million grant due to the exclusion of Marie Stopes International.

APPENDIX. UNFPA ADMINISTRATION POLICY AND LEGISLATIVE CONDITIONS, FY1985 TO FY2011

Fiscal Year	Administration Budget Request	Congressional Action/Legislative Conditions Enacted	Funding and Policy Outcome
1985	$26 million for UNFPA.	**Regular FY1985 appropriation:** —Not less than $46 million, or 16% of Population Assistance, whichever is lower, shall be made available for UNFPA. ** **Supplemental FY1985 appropriation:** —Kemp-Kasten conditions first enacted.	UNFPA received $36 million, after the withholding of $10 million to express U.S. disapproval of coercion in China's family planning program.
1986	$38 million for UNFPA.	—Kemp-Kasten conditions. —No specific UNFPA provision.	No UNFPA funding.
1987	$32 million for UNFPA, subject to Kemp-Kasten.	—Kemp-Kasten conditions. —No specific UNFPA provision.	No UNFPA funding.
1988	$25 million for UNFPA, subject to Kemp-Kasten.	—Kemp-Kasten conditions. —No specific UNFPA provision.	No UNFPA funding
1989	$20 million for UNFPA, subject to Kemp-Kasten.	—Kemp-Kasten conditions. —No specific UNFPA provision.	No UNFPA funding.
1990	$19.39 million for UNFPA, subject to Kemp-Kasten.	Appropriation passed Congress but vetoed by the President: —Not less than $15 million shall be made available for UNFPA, notwithstanding the Kemp-Kasten conditions. —No funds for UNFPA may be used in China. —No UNFPA funds available unless UNFPA maintains amounts in a separate account and UNFPA does not commingle amounts with other sums.	No UNFPA funding Earlier, $15 million appropriation for UNFPA vetoed by the President.

Fiscal Year	Administration Budget Request	Congressional Action/Legislative Conditions Enacted	Funding and Policy Outcome
		—Entire $15 million shall be refunded if any used by UNFPA for family planning programs in China or used for any abortion related activity in any country. *************************************** Subsequent appropriation signed by the President: —Kemp-Kasten conditions. —No specific UNFPA provision.	
1991	$10 million for UNFPA, subject to Kemp-Kasten	—Kemp-Kasten conditions. —No specific UNFPA provision.	No UNFPA funding
1992	$10 million for UNFPA, subject to Kemp-Kasten.	—Kemp-Kasten conditions. —No specific UNFPA provision.	No UNFPA funding
1993	No UNFPA funding.	—Kemp-Kasten conditions. —No specific UNFPA provision.	No UNFPA funding.
1994	$50 million for UNFPA.	—Not more than $40 million shall be made available for UNFPA, subject to Kemp-Kasten conditions. —No funds for UNFPA may be used in China. —No UNFPA funds available unless UNFPA maintains amounts in a separate account and does not commingle amounts with other sums. —Not more than half of the UNFPA contribution may be provided before March 1, 1994. —Secretary of State report to Congress by Feb. 15, 1994, regarding the amount of UNFPA's budget for China. Whatever amount for China above $10 million shall be deducted after March 1 from the $40 million U.S. contribution.	UNFPA received $40 million from the United States.

(Continued)

Fiscal Year	Administration Budget Request	Congressional Action/Legislative Conditions Enacted	Funding and Policy Outcome
1995	$60 million for UNFPA.	—Not more than $50 million shall be made available for UNFPA, subject to Kemp-Kasten conditions. —No funds for UNFPA may be used in China. —No UNFPA funds available unless UNFPA maintains amounts in a separate account and does not commingle amounts with other sums. —Not more than half of the UNFPA contribution may be provided before March 1, 1995. —Secretary of State report to Congress by Feb. 15, 1995, regarding the amount of UNFPA's budget for China. Whatever amount for China above $7 million shall be deducted after March 1 from the $50 million U.S. contribution. ************************************** —In separate legislation, Congress rescinded $15 million of the original $50 million appropriation for UNFPA.	UNFPA received $35 million from the United States, after a rescission of $15 million.
1996	$55 million for UNFPA.	—Not more than $30 million shall be made available for UNFPA, subject to Kemp-Kasten conditions. —No funds for UNFPA may be used in China. —No UNFPA funds available unless UNFPA maintains amounts in a separate account and does not commingle amounts with other sums. —Not more than half of the UNFPA contribution may be provided before March 1, 1996. —Secretary of State report to Congress by Feb. 15, 1996, regarding the amount of UNFPA's budget for China. Whatever amount for China above $7 million shall be deducted after March 1 from the $30 million U.S. contribution.	UNFPA received $22.8 million from the United States, after a withholding of $7.2 million.

Fiscal Year	Administration Budget Request	Congressional Action/Legislative Conditions Enacted	Funding and Policy Outcome
1997	$30 million for NFPA.	—Not more than $25 million shall be made available for UNFPA, subject to Kemp-Kasten conditions. —No funds for UNFPA may be used in China. —No UNFPA funds available unless UNFPA maintains amounts in a separate account and does not commingle amounts with other sums. —Not more than half of the UNFPA contribution may be provided before March 1, 1997. —Secretary of State report to Congress by Feb. 15, 1997, regarding the amount of UNFPA's budget for China. Whatever amount for China shall be deducted after March 1 from the $25 million U.S. contribution.	UNFPA received $25 million from the United States.
1998	$30 million for UNFPA.	—Not more than $25 million shall be made available for UNFPA, subject to Kemp-Kasten conditions. —No funds for UNFPA may be used in China. No UNFPA funds available unless UNFPA maintains amounts in a separate account and does not commingle amounts with other sums. —Not more than half of the UNFPA contribution may be provided before March 1, 1998. —Secretary of State report to Congress by Feb. 15, 1998, regarding the amount of UNFPA's budget for China. Whatever amount for China shall be deducted after March1 from the $25 million U.S. contribution.	UNFPA received $20 million from the United States, after a withholding of $5 million.
1999	$25 million for UNFPA.	—No funds may be made available for UNFPA. —Kemp-Kasten conditions included in enacted appropriation.	UNFPA received no funding from the United States.
2000	$25 million for UNFPA.	—Not more than $25 million shall be made available for UNFPA, subject to Kemp-Kasten conditions. —No funds for UNFPA may be used in China. —No UNFPA funds available unless UNFPA maintains amounts in a separate account, does not commingle amounts with other sums, and does not fund abortions.	UNFPA received $21.5 million from the United States, after a with-holding of $3.5 million.

(Continued)

Fiscal Year	Administration Budget Request	Congressional Action/Legislative Conditions Enacted	Funding and Policy Outcome
		—Secretary of State report to Congress by Feb. 15, 2000, regarding the amount of UNFPA's budget for China. Whatever amount for China shall be deducted after March 1 from the $25 million U.S. contribution.	
2001	$25 million for UNFPA.	—Not more than $25 million shall be made available for UNFPA, subject to Kemp-Kasten conditions. —No funds for UNFPA may be used in China. —No UNFPA funds available unless UNFPA maintains amounts in a separate account, does not commingle amounts with other sums, and does not fund abortions. —Secretary of State report to Congress by Feb. 15, 2001, regarding the amount of UNFPA's budget for China. Whatever amount for China shall be deducted after March 1 from the $25 million U.S. contribution.	UNFPA received $21.5 million from the United States, after a withholding of $3.5 million.
2002	$25 million for UNFPA.	—Not more than $34 million shall be made available for UNFPA, subject to Kemp-Kasten conditions. —No funds for UNFPA may be used in China. —No UNFPA funds available unless UNFPA maintains amounts in a separate account, does not commingle amounts with other sums, and does not fund abortions.	Secretary of State determined that UNFPA was not eligible under Kemp-Kasten conditions. UNFPA received no funding from the United States. FY2002 UNFPA funds reprogrammed for bilateral family planning/ maternal & re-productive health activities in several developing countries.

Fiscal Year	Administration Budget Request	Congressional Action/Legislative Conditions Enacted	Funding and Policy Outcome
2003	$25 million "reserve" available for UNFPA, subject to Kemp-Kasten conditions.	—Not more than $34 million in FY2002 appropriations and an equal amount from FY2003 appropriations shall be available for UNFPA if the President determines that UNFPA no longer supports or participates in the management of a program of coercive abortion or involuntary sterilization. —No funds for UNFPA may be used in China. —Other abortion restrictions in this act or in the FY2002 appropriation shall apply to UNFPA funding. —FY2002 conditions on UNFPA funding shall apply to FY2003 appropriations. —UNFPA funds deducted by the amount UNFPA spends in China in 2002 and 2003.	President did not issue a finding that UNFPA no longer supports or participates in the management of a program of coercive abortion or involuntary sterilization. UNFPA received no funding from the United States. FY2003 UNFPA funds reprogrammed for assistance for "vulnerable children" and made available for a new initiative for assistance for
2004	$25 million reserve available for UNFPA, subject to Kemp-Kasten conditions.	—Up to $34 million shall be available to UNFPA, subject to Kemp-Kasten conditions. —FY2002 UNFPA funds shall be made available for family planning, maternal & reproductive health activities in the Democratic Republic of the Congo, Ethiopia, Nigeria, Tanzania, Uganda, Haiti, Georgia, Azerbaijan, Russia, Albania, Romania, and Kazakhstan. —FY2003 UNFPA funds shall be allocated for assistance for "vulnerable children" and made available for a new initiative for assistance for young women, mothers and children who are victims of trafficking in persons. —No UNFPA funds available for programs in China. —No UNFPA funds available unless UNFPA maintains amounts in a separate account, does not commingle amounts with other sums, and UNFPA does not fund abortions.	Secretary of State determined that UNFPA was not eligible under Kemp-Kasten conditions. UNFPA received no funding from the United States.

(Continued)

Fiscal Year	Administration Budget Request	Congressional Action/Legislative Conditions Enacted	Funding and Policy Outcome
			FY2004 UNFPA funds transferred to the Economic Support Fund account, with the intention to use in support of anti-trafficking in persons programs. Subsequently, FY2005 Foreign Operations Appropriations directed that of the FY2004 funds not provided to UNFPA, $12.5 million shall be available for anti-trafficking programs, and $12.5 million shall be available for AID family planning programs.
2005	$25 million reserve available for UNFPA, subject to Kemp-Kasten conditions.	—$34 million shall be available to UNFPA, subject to Kemp-Kasten conditions. —No UNFPA funds available for programs in China. —No UNFPA funds available unless UNFPA maintains amounts in a separate account, does not commingle amounts with other sums, and UNFPA does not fund abortions. —If FY2005 funds are not made available to UNFPA, they shall be transferred to the Child Survival/Health account and used by USAID for family planning, maternal, and reproductive health activities.	Secretary of State determined that UNFPA was not eligible under Kemp-Kasten conditions. UNFPA received no funding from the United States.

Fiscal Year	Administration Budget Request	Congressional Action/Legislative Conditions Enacted	Funding and Policy Outcome
		—Of the FY2004 funds earmarked for UNFPA, $12.5 million shall be available for anti-trafficking programs and $12.5 million shall be available for USAID for family planning, maternal, and reproductive health activities in Albania, Azerbaijan, the Democratic Republic of the Congo, Ethiopia, Georgia, Haiti, Kazakhstan, Kenya, Nigeria, Romania, Russia, Rwanda, Tanzania, Uganda, and Ukraine.	
2006	If UNFPA determined eligible for U.S. funds under the terms of Kemp-Kasten, $25 0	—$34 million shall be available to UNFPA, subject to Kemp-Kasten conditions. —No UNFPA funds available for programs in China. —No UNFPA funds available unless UNFPA maintains amounts in a separate account, does not commingle amounts with other sums, and UNFPA does not fund	Secretary of State determined that UNFPA was not eligible under
	million could be drawn from USAID's Child Survival and Health Account.	abortions. —Of the $34 million, $22.5 million shall be derived from the State Department's International Organization and Programs account (IOP), with the remainder from the Child Survival and Health account (CSH). —Of the amount derived from the IOP account that are not made available for UNFPA, the funds shall be transferred to the CSH account, and shall be made available for family planning, and maternal and reproductive health services.	Kemp-Kasten conditions. UNFPA received no funding from the United States.
2007	If UNFPA determined eligible for U.S. funds under the terms of Kemp-Kasten, $25 million could Be drawn from the proposed family planning/ reproductive health program budget of $357 million.	**Per H.R. 5522, Foreign Operations, Export Financing, and Related Programs Appropriations Bill:** —$34 million shall be available to UNFPA, subject to Kemp-Kasten conditions. —No UNFPA funds available for programs in China. —No UNFPA funds available unless UNFPA maintains amounts in a separate account, does not commingle amounts with other sums, and UNFPA does not fund abortions.	Pending under continuing resolution P.L. 109-289, as amended by P.L. 110-5 Secretary of State determined that UNFPA was not eligible under Kemp-Kasten conditions. UNFPA received no funding from the United States.

(Continued)

Fiscal Year	Administration Budget Request	Congressional Action/Legislative Conditions Enacted	Funding and Policy Outcome
		—Of the $34 million, $22.275 million shall be derived from the State Department's IOP account, with the remainder from the Child Survival and Health account (CSH). —Of the amount derived from the IOP account that are not made available for UNFPA, the funds shall be transferred to the CSH account, and shall be made available for family planning, and maternal and reproductive health services.	
2008	If UNFPA is determined eligible for U.S. funds under the terms of Kemp-Kasten, $25 million would be drawn from the Child Survival and Health Programs account.	—$40 million shall be available to UNFPA, subject to Kemp-Kasten conditions. —No UNFPA funds available for programs in China. —No UNFPA funds available unless UNFPA maintains amounts in a separate account, does not commingle amounts with other sums, and UNFPA does not fund abortions. —Not less than $7 million shall be derived from funding appropriated under the IOP, with the rest coming from the Global Health and Child Survival account. —Of the amount derived from the IOP account that are not made available for UNFPA, the funds shall be transferred to the Global Health and Child Survival account, and shall be made available for family planning and maternal and reproductive health activities.	Secretary of State determined that UNFPA is not eligible under Kemp-Kasten conditions. UNFPA will receive no funding from the United States.
		—Report to Congress and Dollar-for-Dollar Withholding of Funds: No later than four months after enactment, the Secretary of State shall report to Appropriations Committees on the "amount of funds that UNFPA is budgeting for the year in which the report is submitted for a country program in the People's Republic of China."	

Fiscal Year	Administration Budget Request	Congressional Action/Legislative Conditions Enacted	Funding and Policy Outcome
		If a report indicates that UNFPA plans to spend funds for a country program in China in the year of the report, the amount of funds that UNFPA plans to spend in China shall be deducted from the funds made available to UNFPA after March 1 for obligation for the rest of the fiscal year. Moreover, nothing shall be construed to limit the authority of the President to deny funds to any organization due to the application of another law or provision. —Requires the Administration to make Kemp-Kasten determinations within six months of the enactment of the act, and directs that the decision must be accompanied by "a comprehensive analysis as well as the complete evidence and criteria utilized to make the determination."	
2009	If UNFPA is determined eligible for U.S. funds under the terms of Kemp-Kasten, $25 million would be drawn from the Child Survival and Health Programs account.	—$50 million shall be made available to UNFPA, subject to Kemp-Kasten provisions, of which not more than $30 million will be derived from the International Organization and Programs account. —Funds appropriated to UNFPA that are not made available because of the operation of any provision of law, shall be made available to UNFPA "notwithstanding any such provision of law." —Funds for UNFPA shall only be used to: (1) provide and distribute equipment and medicine; (2) make contraceptives available; (3) prevent and treat obstetric fistula; (4) reestablish maternal health services; (5) promote the abandonment of female genital cutting; and (6) promote access to basic services. —No U.S. funds shall be made available to UNFPA unless it maintains U.S. funds in a separate account, does not commingle amounts with other sums, and UNFPA does not fund abortions. —No UNFPA funds shall be made available for a UNFPA country program in China.	UNFPA received an estimated $50 million from the United States.

(Continued)

Fiscal Year	Administration Budget Request	Congressional Action/Legislative Conditions Enacted	Funding and Policy Outcome
		—No later than 60 days after the enactment of the act, the Secretary is required to submit a report to the Committees on Appropriations indicating the funds UNFPA is budgeting for a country program in China. If the Secretary's report indicates that funds will be spent a China program, then the amount of such funds shall be deducted from the funds made available to UNFPA after March 1 for obligation for the remainder of the fiscal year in which the report is submitted.	
2010	$50 million, drawn from the International Organizations and Programs account.	—$55 million shall be made available to UNFPA, subject to Kemp-Kasten provisions. Funds will be derived from the International Organization and Programs account. —Funds appropriated for UNFPA that are not made available for UNFPA because of the operation of any provision of law, shall be transferred to the Global Health and Child Survival account and shall be made available for family planning, maternal, and reproductive health activities. —None of the funds made available may be used by UNFPA for a country program in the People's Republic of China. —Funds made available for UNFPA may not be made available unless: (1) UNFPA maintains funds in an account separate from other accounts of UNFPA and does not commingle such funds with other sums; and (2) UNFPA does not fund abortions. —Not later than four months after the date of enactment of the act, the Secretary of State shall submit a report to the Committees on Appropriations indicating the amount of funds that the UNFPA is budgeting for the year in which the report is submitted for a country program in China.	UNFPA received an estimated $55 million from the United States

Fiscal Year	Administration Budget Request	Congressional Action/Legislative Conditions Enacted	Funding and Policy Outcome
		If the report indicates that UNFPA plans to spend funds for a country program in China in the year covered by the report, then the amount of such funds the UNFPA plans to spend in China shall be deducted from the funds made available to the UNFPA after March 1 for obligation for the remainder of the fiscal year in which the report is submitted.	
2011	$50 million, drawn from the International Organizations and Programs account.	To be determined.	To be determined.

End Notes

[1] *UNFPA: What it Is; What it Does*, UNFPA, 1983; and "UNFPA at 30 Years—Fact Sheets," UNFPA, October 26, 1999. (Hereafter cited as UNFPA, What it Is; What it Does.)

[2] *UNFPA. What it Is; What it Does*, 1983.

[3] See CRS Report 94-533, *Population and Development: The 1994 Cairo Conference*, by Curt Tarnoff (out of print; available on request from the author).

[4] UNFPA background, at http://www.unfpa.org/hiv/index.htm.

[5] *UNFPA Annual Report 2009*, at http://www.unfpa.org/public/home/publications/pid/6057.

[6] Obstetric fistula occurs from prolonged child labor, particularly when labor lasts two days or more. When a woman or girl is unable to push her baby out, the pressure from the baby's head can interrupt blood flow to tissues in the pelvic area. Ultimately, the woman passes the baby after it dies, as the decomposed body is smaller than the live one. This can cause incontinence, nerve damage, and chronic pain, which can make walking difficult. For more information on UNFPA activities regarding fistula, see CRS Report RS21773, *Reproductive Health Problems in the World: Obstetric Fistula: Background Information and Responses*, by Tiaji Salaam-Blyther.

[7] For more information on UNFPA activities and areas of focus, see http://www.unfpa.org/public /about.

[8] *UNFPA Annual Report 2008* and *Annual Report* 2009. Additional data also drawn from prior-year annual reports. UNFPA's 2010 annual report has not yet been published.

[9] U.S. Congress. Senate Committee on Foreign Relations. *Foreign Assistance Act of 1967; report to accompany S. 1872*. S.Rept. 90-499. August 9, 1967, p. 24.

[10] U.S. Agency for International Development. Development and Humanitarian Assistance; FY1973 Program Presentation to Congress. p. L-15.

[11] For a discussion of the Mexico City policy and its eligibility requirements, see CRS Report RL30830, *International Family Planning: The "Mexico City" Policy*, by Larry Nowels.

[12] More recently, responsibility for UNFPA voluntary contributions has shifted to the State Department and the Bureau of Population, Refugees, and Migration.

[13] Action Memorandum for the Administrator/Acting Director of IDCA. *1985 Funding for the United Nations Fund for Population Activities (UNFPA)*, September 25, 1985, p. 1.

[14] Ibid.

[15] Initially, the amendment was referred to as the Kemp-Inouye provision, so named after its original sponsors, Representative Jack Kemp, ranking Member of the House Foreign Assistance Appropriations Subcommittee, and Senator Daniel Inouye, Ranking Member of the Senate Foreign Assistance Appropriations Subcommittee. Senator Inouye later opposed the Administration's decision not to fund UNFPA, as well as the fact that the decision was delegated from the President to the Secretary of State to the Administrator for USAID. For the next several years, Senator Bob Kasten, Chairman/Ranking Minority Member of the Foreign Assistance Subcommittee, was a strong supporter of the amendment, and the provision came to be referred to as "Kemp-Kasten."

[16] S.Amdt. 338 to H.R. 2577, 99th Congress, June 20, 1985. Enacted as P.L. 99-88.

[17] U.S. House. Committee on Appropriations. Supplemental Appropriations, *1985*, H.Rept. 99-142, May 22, 1985, p. 86.

[18] Ibid.

[19] A USAID memorandum drafted at the time noted that the Administration did not view congressional expectations that the President (or if delegated, the Secretary of State) should make the determination for UNFPA funding as legally binding. However, it was "considered significant" by the executive branch.

[20] IDCA had been established by Congress as a government entity to oversee and coordinate the activities of all U.S. foreign aid agencies, and the IDCA Director served simultaneously as the USAID Administrator.

[21] Letter from IDCA Acting Director Peter McPherson to Senator Hatfield, Chairman of the Senate Appropriations Committee, September 25, 1985, p. 2.

[22] Ibid, p. 2.

[23] These policy views are drawn from letters of USAID Administrator Brian Atwood to Senator Helms, dated August 6 and September 10, 1993.

[24] Senate Committee on Foreign Relations, *U.S. Funding for the U.N. Population Fund: The Effect on Women's Lives*. Committee Hearings, February 2002.

[25] *Report of the China UN Population Fund (UNFPA) Independent Assessment Team,* released by the Department of State on May 29, 2002. See http://www.state.gov/g/prm/rls/rpt/2002 /12122.htm for the report's full text.

[26] In 2008, for example, a Bush Administration official stated, "We are prepared to consider funding UNFPA in the future if its program in China is ended or restructured in a way consistent with U.S. law, or if China ends its program of coercive abortion and involuntary sterilization." See press statement by Tom Casey, Deputy Spokesman, "Fiscal Year 2008 Funding for the United Nations Population Fund (UNFPA)," U.S. Department of State, June 27, 2008.

[27] Department of State, *Analysis of Determination that Kemp-Kasten Amendment Precludes Further Funding to UNFPA under P.L. 107-115.* Released on July 18, 2002.

[28] Department of State press release, "U.S. Government Support for the United Nations Population Fund (UNFPA)," March 24, 2009.

[29] Congressional Budget Justification, Foreign Operations, FY2011, U.S. Department of State, pp. 132, 161-162.

[30] Congressional Budget Justification, Foreign Operations, FY2010, U.S. Department of State, pp. 27, 91, 193.

[31] The bill also established related reporting requirements for the Secretary-of-State. No later than 60 days after the enactment of P.L. 111-8, the Secretary was required to submit a report to the Committees on Appropriations indicating the funds UNFPA budgeted for a country program in China. If the Secretary's report indicated that funds would be spent on such a program, then the amount of such funds should be deducted from the funds made available to UNFPA for the remainder of the fiscal year in which the report was submitted. (See Sec. 7079(e)(1) and (e)(2).)

[32] Appendix, Congressional Budget Justification, Foreign Operations, FY2009, p. 815, available at http://www.whitehouse.gov/omb/budget/FY2009/pdf/appendix/sta.pdf.

[33] UNFPA, *Country Programme Outline for China.* DP/FPA/CPO/CHN/5*, July 12, 2002. UNFPA, *Report of the International Review Team on the UNFPA China Country Programme,* October 2001.

[34] UNFPA, *Country Programme Document for China.* DP/FPA/CPD/CHN/6, October 10, 2005.

[35] Population Research Institute, *UNFPA, China, and Coercive Family Planning.* December 12, 2001. See also two congressional hearings in which Josephine Guy testified: House Committee on International Relations, *Coercive Population Control in China: New Evidence of Foreign Abortion and Forced Sterilization.* Committee Hearing, October 17, 2001; and Senate Committee on Foreign Relations, *U.S. Funding for the U.N. Population Fund: The Effect on Women's Lives.* Committee Hearings, February 2002.

[36] UNFPA, *Report of the International Review Team on the UNFPA China Country Programme,* October 2001. Senate Committee on Foreign Relations, *U.S. Funding for the U.N. Population Fund: The Effect on Women's Lives.* Committee Hearings, February 2002.

[37] China Mission Report by UK MP's, 1st April - 9th April 2002. Found at http://www.appg-popdevrh.org.uk.

[38] Catholics for a Free Choice. *The United Nations Population Fund in China: A Catalyst for Change.* Report of an Interfaith Delegation to China. 2003.

[39] Christopher Marquis, "U.S. is Accused of Trying to Isolate U.N. Population Unit," *New York Times,* June 21, 2004. Letter to Secretary of State Colin Powell from Representatives Maloney, Lee, Waxman, and Crowley, June 18, 2004.

[40] *Details for Funding the Reproductive Health Consortium (Taken Question)*, Office of the State Department's Spokesman, August 27, 2003.

INDEX

A

B

C

D

E

S

T

U

V